BLUE PAWS

BLUE PAWS

MATT McCREDIE

NEW
HOLLAND

Contents

To every past and present Operational Police Dog Handler and their dogs.
I hope this book does all of you justice.

Acknowledgments

Mike Bailey who recently passed away. Thank you for encouraging me to continue on and finish what I started. Greg Judkins who kept my head on straight when I could easily have lost it. All of my close and extended family and friends, especially my very beautiful and equally understanding wife Enza.

Last but not least, Merlin, because without you none of this would have been possible.

Foreword

I have been in law enforcement for over thirty years and of those thirty years I have been a dog handler for the New South Wales Police for twenty.

In 1989 the Dog Squad was regionalised into four regions. In 1998, we amalgamated back to the one dog unit. It was at the amalgamation of these four separate regions that I first met Matt. From the time I met him until now, he has not changed. He is somewhat larger than life, with an enthusiasm and passion for his work that can sometimes overpower others with lesser enthusiasm. This passion and enthusiasm carries over in to other aspects of his life, his family and his other passions—motorbikes and rugby.

Being a dog handler in the dog unit is unlike any other job. It is a lifestyle. All dog handlers and their sometimes suffering families realise the job doesn't finish at the end of the shift. The dog still needs to be fed, cared for and bedded down before the handler can take care of himself. This also applies on rest days and annual leave.

Matt is one of those policemen who love to get involved. The more dangerous or bizarre, the more he relishes it. This trait makes for a good worker and dog handler. As his supervisor, I know he goes to everything and anything where he may be able to assist or use his police dog. I have had both the pleasure and the pain of having Matt on my team.

I'm sure he won't mind me saying that as well as doing some good police work, he can make his supervisor earn his money too. At the end of the day, I would still have a few more like him and I certainly would like to have him and his dog backing me up on the street.

Sergeant Roger Mayer
Sydney, NSW

Introduction

My name is Matt McCredie and I am a serving police officer with the New South Wales Police Dog Squad. I joined the police in 1991 and have served as a frontline officer since graduating from the academy. I performed general duties at City Central, Surry Hills, Redfern and Chatswood police stations. I have also performed duties in plain clothes at the then City East Anti-theft Unit and the Northern Suburbs Anti-theft Unit with a final short stint at the City East Transit Police. Over this time I have served with many fine police officers who have worn the uniform with the same pride and professionalism that I have. Hopefully this book will illustrate just what it's like to be a modern day police officer.

I marched into the New South Wales Police Academy in early 1991 after spending the previous three years working as a prison officer at Long Bay Correctional Centre. I'd had about a week's rest then headed straight to Goulburn. The Goulburn Police Academy is located on the Southern Tablelands of New South Wales and is a major rural centre. It's not exactly a beautiful holiday destination but it's not a Siberian gulag either. The Academy is there to serve a purpose and that is to produce the best possible police officers for this state.

Almost straight away I was in trouble. I had come from a maximum-security prison where every second word you hear is a profanity. I had unfortunately brought some of that with me and it wasn't until one of the instructors recorded me answering a question in class that I realised I had some work to do. The instructors helped me out and it wasn't long until I had lost my gaol habit.

Being a prison officer had one great advantage in that it had given me a very good insight into the criminal world and mind. I remember one of the bosses out at Long Bay once told me, 'you will learn more about psychology in here in a week than you would in a year at university.' I got to meet many infamous criminals during my time at Long Bay. The most interesting person who really gave me an insight into what criminals think of police was Jockey Smith. He was a career criminal who specialised in armed robberies. I got to know him and had quite a few long conversations with him while I was helping to run the wing that he was living in, so much so that I would call him Jockey and he would call me Matt. However this came to a very abrupt end when he found out that I had been accepted into the police. Such was his hatred of police that he shook his head and never spoke to me again. Not that I really care, but it was amazing to see how black and white some criminals see things. Most of the time, working in a prison is very, very boring. The money was great but I just couldn't take the sheer boredom of sitting around watching criminals constantly arguing with criminals about the same things and being confined behind the same walls day in and day out, so I joined the police.

Just like at school, I found the studying a complete bore and the physical activities and practical policing lessons great fun. After six months, I finally graduated as a probationary constable. I couldn't wait to get into my new career for real. This was fourteen years ago and things were a bit different in the police then. Some things were bad and some were good. The people who joined were a bit different as well. There were a lot of knock-about blokes and not nearly as many university graduates entering the force as there are now. I remember walking into a certain Sydney District Police Station on my first day. I walked in with my immaculate uniform on and went to the front counter where there was a very large and happy looking sergeant standing there eyeballing me. He told me to come around to where he was standing. I happily walked around and stood in front of him. He told me to come closer then started to explain to me that as a probationary constable I was at a level just below a police dog and would have to work very hard to get myself up past the very low level I was currently occupying. He kept the big smile on his face then shook my hand welcoming me to 'The Job'. He would turn out to be a great mentor who I respected and learned a great deal from. Little did I know that in years to come when I started to train as a dog handler I would return to that low level just below the rank of police dog and have to work extremely hard to get up past it again.

Like I said, the police force was a very different world in those days and a lot has changed. That kind of humour and larrikinism isn't as prevalent as it used to be.

Anyway I spent my time at a lot of different police stations within the City District of Sydney, most of it at the Redfern Patrol and the Sydney District Anti-theft Squad. It was these two places that really shaped my policing.

Redfern

Redfern was and still is a very in-your-face policing environment. Percentages of the local population don't like the police and don't care if they break the law. I remember at one stage, out of about twenty police vehicles at Redfern, only one had no damage to it. All the others had smashed windows, slashed tyres, battered panels and broken aerials. This is where I learned to never assume anything.

I was working on Redfern 1, which was the patrol's caged truck. It was about 2am on a weekday and we had been called to Eveleigh Street, Redfern, to recover a stolen vehicle. We drove down and noticed that everything was very quiet. Usually there are people walking around. As we pulled up behind the stolen car, I saw a car pull up down the bottom of the street blocking it off. Then I heard screeching tyres at the top of the street and another car did the same thing. To paint the picture, we were trapped. There was no way we could get our truck out of there. Then it started. We were pelted with bottles and bricks, hundreds of them, including full house bricks and glass bottles full of sand. My partner and I jumped back into the truck, which was by now bearing the full brunt of the attack. All the windows were smashed and the police radio was not working. It sounded like a hailstorm on a tin roof. I was getting worried. My partner who was much more senior to me said, 'Get your baton and follow me.' These were the days before capsicum spray. He had retrieved our portable police radio and called for assistance. We ran out of the truck and straight into the half-demolished terrace houses where the barrage was coming from. He yelled to me, 'Move anything or anyone that gets in your way.' On the way in, bricks hit our bodies and I copped one beauty to the side of the head. Luckily it's quite thick so there wasn't much damage.

We ran into the pitch black where I could hear voices and movement. There were screams of, 'Kill the bastards!' and other choice comments. I have to admit I was very concerned about my physical wellbeing by this stage. I ran into a couple of bodies while trying to get through and I hit them with my baton very hard. Both went down in screaming heaps. I wasn't going to stop to make an arrest we had neither the time nor means to make. At the time I really thought we were fighting for our lives. I kept going and eventually came out on Caroline Street, which is right near the railway station. I could hear sirens and see plenty of police wearing riot gear (at the time Redfern was one of only a few police stations to have riot equipment on constant hand and readiness) heading down to where our vehicle had been left.

I found my partner covered in blood from a cut to his head but smiling back at me. We were both about to go back down when our shift supervisor grabbed us and sent us to hospital. I was in no mood for that, knowing that there was a running street battle going on and no way was I going to let someone else do all the work. After a few small but highly violent encounters, order was restored and our vehicle recovered. It had been found on its side with just about every panel and window destroyed. The mob had tried to set it on fire but had been unable to get their oily rag far enough into the petrol tank. The interior was slashed and ripped way beyond repair. I learned that things aren't always as they seem and never to assume that because it looks safe the street is safe. I spent three good years at Redfern making some good friends and learning a lot about policing. I'm grateful that I was sent to a busy station to start my career. I learned a hell of a lot more than those who were sent to much quieter areas.

Anti-Theft

I was lucky enough to go on a secondment to the then Sydney District Anti-theft Squad for twelve months. In this section you wear everyday clothes and sneak around doing various plain clothes jobs. It's always great fun when you grab a criminal who asks you who the hell you are, then you flash the badge and make the arrest. I'll talk about two incidents which stand out. One of the most nerve-wracking jobs I ever did was in this section. The Major Crime Squad was doing an operation in Kings Cross using undercover police to buy drugs, then arrest the dealers. This had been going on for about a week with our section helping with search warrants and arrests of these dealers. All the trained UCs (undercover police) had been used but there were still a few targets who needed attention. They turned to us and asked who wanted to have a go at being a UC and buy some drugs. Like I said, things have changed a lot since. These days there is a dedicated course to be taken before you can perform these duties. I was full of self-confidence and wasn't worried about the consequences of getting it wrong.

I thought, you beauty, this sounds like fun and stuck up my hand. I should have looked around a bit harder and noticed that none of the senior guys had put up their hands. Anyway, I was given a few instructions, some marked money and away I went with about ten other police watching me. I sat down outside the Amsterdam Café in Kings Cross and only had to wait about three minutes until a grubby little man came up and asked whether I wanted to score any drugs. I said 'yeah' and came up with a story that I was from Melbourne and didn't really know my way around. He gathered a couple of other buyers and we walked up to a certain pub on Darlinghurst Road. All the time I was getting more and more nervous. I was smoking heavily and could feel the sweat running down my back, all the time hoping that none of the others came from Melbourne and were going to quiz me. I don't know how the full time guys do it without going over the edge. I have the utmost respect for undercover police.

Eventually we made it to the hotel and I even managed to get the dealer to come out and do the deal on the street. I almost laughed out loud when he said that he didn't like doing it out here because there were a lot of police about. I grabbed the grass out of his hand and shoved my cash back in. Then out of nowhere the police came in and arrested the lot of us. It had been a good victory because we recovered a lot of cash and drugs from his hotel room but the mental strain was quite high.

The second job was one of those that came from absolutely nowhere. This is one of the best things about being a police officer, one minute it's boring and mundane, then the next it's on for young and old. It was a Monday morning about 8am and I was driving with Greg. We were looking at a suspected drug dealer's house on Abercrombie Street in Chippendale. This is a high density living area close to the centre of Sydney. I just happened to look to my right and saw an old Sigma sedan turn right with three people on board. The car had turned a little fast which made me a bit suspicious. I reefed the wheel, turning our unmarked Commodore around and following at a distance. In an effort to hide our identity, I eased up behind the Sigma instead of rushing up quickly. It worked and we followed the car through a few back streets and out onto Elizabeth Street, finally watching as the car stopped outside a methadone clinic. All this just as the call came back from the police radio confirming that this was a stolen car. I pulled up beside it and looked straight at the passenger and driver who picked me straight away. The driver was about twenty years old. In the front was a passenger about forty years old, and the rear passenger was a young girl of about eighteen years. They all looked very surprised. The driver put the Sigma straight into gear and floored it up onto the footpath. Luckily there were no pedestrians around at the time. Greg called the pursuit over the police radio, 'Alpha 21 urgent we are in pursuit of that stolen vehicle.'

We chased the Sigma west on Broadway near Central Railway Station, weaving in and out of the peak hour traffic with this lunatic mounting the kerb again while turning south onto Abercrombie Street. Abercrombie Street is a one-way four-lane road, with the traffic flowing north. Luckily one of the motorists stopped at the lights in front of us moved over and let us through. It was at this stage that a couple of things happened. First Greg lost his faith in my driving skills. He turned to me and said, 'Matt, please don't do this.' I answered, 'Sorry mate it's too late.' I had made the turn and was able to drive up the empty bus lane while the crooks weaved in and out of the oncoming vehicles being driven by bug-eyed motorists. The second thing was that I heard another siren and saw a fully marked Highway Patrol vehicle pull up beside then pass in front of us. Just as we came to the end of the one-way street the police radio operator called us to 'terminate' the pursuit. The Sigma crossed Cleveland Street and was t-boned by another car, spraying broken glass and impacted car panels into the air. This did not stop them and they continued on into a side street. We had backed off and turned off all our lights and sirens. I was disappointed but the danger to the public was too great and the correct decision to terminate had been made.

I drove into the side street that the Sigma had disappeared into to see that it had crashed head on into a brick wall. The driver ran past our car while I watched a member of the public tackle the rear passenger. I couldn't see the front passenger anywhere. I jumped out and took after the driver who was like a jack rabbit. It was the middle of the football season so I was at a good level of fitness and was just able to keep him in sight as we ducked and weaved through the narrow lanes and alleys found all over this part of Sydney. As he rounded a corner onto Cleveland Street I lost sight of him but heard a lot of shouting. Puffing and cursing to myself I came around to find the driver flat on his face being handcuffed by the same highway patrol officer who had driven the pursuit. The driver had run through all these back alleys to lose me and come out right where he had started from and into the arms of my new best friend. 'Mate, you run as good as you drive,' I told him. He was taken back along with his girlfriend and charged. The next day I went to an address they had supplied and arrested the passenger, also charging him with being carried in a stolen vehicle.

I had a great time in the Anti-theft Squad and learnt a lot from some of the state's best police. These are the people who helped me get to where I always wanted to be. There are many more stories I could tell about that journey but this book is about the best job, mate and colleague in the world. It is about the four years that I have spent with Police Dog Merlin. Ever since the first day we were introduced and formed into a dog team there hasn't been a day that I did not want to put him in the back of our police car and go out on the road. There aren't very many people that can boast that kind of job satisfaction.

The Dog Squad

Very briefly, the New South Wales Police Dog Squad was first formed in 1932 under the command of Scotty Denholm. He had a great many successes with a small number of dogs and handlers until 1954 when the Unit was disbanded. In 1979 two police officers were sent to the Victorian Dog Training Facility in Melbourne. They returned with two dogs, reactivating this highly effective policing tool. Since then, all training has been conducted in NSW. From 1980 to 1989 the Unit training was based in St Ives in northern Sydney. After that and until 1998, training was conducted at the Police Dog Training Centre in Goulburn. Now all training is based at Menai in southern Sydney where the Squad is now centrally based. The Dog Squad is a specialist section, which directly supports all operational police throughout the state. Becoming a member of this squad is one of the most sought after jobs in the police.

I remember when I was a very junior constable seeing a dog handler at work and thinking that was for me. How hard could it be? This handler's advice to me at the time was, 'Get out there and do the hard yards. Learn as much as you can and gain the experience, then we may consider looking at you.'

So that's what I did. I went to everything and arrested as many criminals as I could but it was another seven years before I was able get a start on a selection course and that was only after pestering the training staff and commander with constant phone calls and reports to let them know I was ready to try out. I think they let me on the course just to shut me up and get me off their backs.

I showed up on the first day at Menai Police Station and straight away, and in no uncertain terms, we were told that this course was only to see if we had what it takes and in no way meant that we were in. We were told that we were competing with each other but to get through the week we would have to work as a team. There were about ten of us for only four positions. We had been selected from hundreds of applications received by the Dog Squad. It was hard to look around the room and think that I had to beat them all and make it look like I was helping them at the same time.

We started with 'a bit of fitness' which involved a distance run then about twenty hill sprints with sit ups and pushups in between. You have to be fit mentally and physically to be a successful dog handler. Of course during all this we were being screamed at and told we were hopeless and totally unsuitable for this kind of work. They were just trying to see who would crack and say that it was too hard and perhaps they had made a mistake coming here. I can remember one torturous morning running up and down some very steep hills for about an hour before we were told that we were heading back to the squad base for a lecture. Thank God for that, I thought. I was in pain and ready to have a nice sit down. About five meters from where we were about to stop running, the trainer turned and broke our hearts. 'Okay, I'm going in for a shower now. You people are going down the hill with the good sergeant here.' He pointed to one of the training instructors who scowled at us and hissed, 'If you don't want to come then get your gear and leave, otherwise start running and come with me.' My heart had sunk to my feet but what could I do except keep on going.

There were only six of us left by this stage. Four had left either by their own choice, injury or they had been asked to leave. We all looked despondently at each other and turned to follow the sergeant who was joyfully running across the road not even looking back to see if we were coming. One of the boys said, 'Well, what else would you rather be doing.' There was a muffled laugh from everyone before we took off as a group following the devil down the hill. If you want to stay in the police with any sanity you need to have a good sense of humour.

This hill is no ordinary hill—it's about 400m from the bottom to the very top and is a gradient of forty five to fifty five degrees. An absolute sadist's paradise. He took us all the way to the bottom, turned straight away and yelled, 'Go' and we pushed and encouraged each other up this bastard of a hill. My legs were absolutely exploding and my breakfast was percolating at the back of my throat. At the top, the sergeant turned and yelled, 'Run back down, turn straight away and sprint back up—if I think you're slacking off then we will be here all day until you all die. Now get back down there and start.' This went on for half an hour with no rest.

One of the strangest things is watching people go about their normal daily business oblivious as you endure your own personal hell wishing you were somewhere else. By the end I was just looking at my feet and going through the motions to get up and down that hill. I think everyone was in the same condition and no one wanted to give the training staff the satisfaction of beating them. Soon after we all very happily returned to the squad's base, had a shower and collapsed in the lecture room. The pressure was not released for one second in here either. We were given lectures on subjects such as the grooming and general care of dogs including the detection of parasites, common problems and how to identify them. We would be given verbal and written tests, sometimes immediately and sometimes half way through another subject. All the time we were being watched and notes taken.

I found out later that some of the more senior staff would ring up police stations where you used to work and ask whoever answered what kind of person you were, whether they liked you, whether you had many enemies at the station, whether you were a hard working officer or just a bludger. I must have had someone answer who thankfully liked me enough to say good things.

The compound was a fenced off area about 100x100m. It was flat and grassed inside and had all the agility gear set up in the centre. This is where we were told to 'play' with a dog. Sounds easy, but it was probably the hardest thing I had ever tried to do. The dog was attached to a fence by his lead and it was my job to make him bark. I had a rubber ring and one of the most disinterested dogs I have ever come across (he was a dog that was deemed unsuitable for police work). I was jumping up and down whooping and shouting but he just looked away then lay down. The purpose of this exercise was to see whether you would give up or keep on persevering. It would also indicate to the staff how interesting you might be for a dog. If you cannot excite a dog or reward a dog with a great play then he is not going to progress properly through his exercises and he will have no real motivation to keep on going. The training staff knew there was no way this dog was ever going to bark. However, they let me go on for about fifteen minutes and by the end I was absolutely exhausted but had not given up. Just to make sure I was having fun, I then had to run ten laps of the compound, which is about 400m around!

Other testing included the group standing in front of a trainer who threw a cricket ball at us at varying speeds and angles and us having to catch it. If you dropped it or didn't try hard enough then you received a physical penalty. This exercise was to see how much hand-eye coordination you had, important for tracking human scent with the dogs. Another important test was finding out how strong your voice was and how well you could give the words of command. These need to be given the same way every time and with absolute authority. You must be able to change your voice in an instant from being unhappy with him to praising him. The training staff took us out into the compound and asked us to give the command 'no' as if we were saying it to a small child who was about to run out into traffic. I walked out and stood about 50m in front of the two dog handlers. I mustered up all my inner strength and belted out a very loud and heartfelt 'NO'. The two testers looked at me with blank faces and said, 'That was rubbish, do it again.' I took a deep breath and, totally abusing my vocal chords screamed out another 'NO' that would have been heard at the top of the Sydney Harbour Bridge. This time they looked at each other, totally ignoring me, and had a conversation which was just loud enough for everybody to hear.

'He's pretty poor and doesn't really have any power in his voice— it's piss weak.'

'Yeah mate, I agree he's got nothing.'

I was told to sit down. I wanted to protest and get them to put on their hearing aids as obviously they hadn't been listening properly. Instead I slinked back and sat down with the group, a little bit demoralised. To make it worse no one said a word or tried to cheer me up. We all just sat there with blank faces. The instructors were playing their game to perfection by encouraging and praising everybody with obviously weaker voices and criticising all those with good, strong voices. This just confused us more and helped to increase our anxiety levels. I still can't believe I fell for their trap hook, line and sinker.

Slowly but surely we were introduced to the dogs which would be on our training course if we made it that far. We would groom them and take them for group walks where we would try to make them walk next to each handler whilst on a lead, not easy when all the dogs wanted to be at the front. However, this was to see how we could communicate to our dog using voice and a choker chain. I developed a sore shoulder and wrist from constantly trying to hold the dogs back. For the first two days they had no regard and certainly no respect for any of us. This changed as the course progressed.

On about the fourth day of the course, we were instructed to remove the course dogs from the kennels and groom them. One officer forgot to check the name on one of the kennel doors and removed a fully trained and very experienced police dog (German shepherd). One thing led to another and needless to say he tried to groom this dog that took exception and attacked him. The officer received numerous cuts and abrasions from the dog who very nearly bit into his jugular. This incident highlighted the fact that these were not backyard pets; they were working dogs who needed to be treated with the utmost respect.

The Dog Squad looks for people who are experienced operational police, have a generally happy and positive disposition, a forceful character, a desire to achieve, are able to work in a team enviroment, and are also able to confidently work on their own. They never give up, are physically fit and are devoted to their duty and dog. Probably most importantly, they have a special and indefinable quality which enables them to communicate and have an affinity with dogs.

There are a lot of very good police officers who have participated in this course and have not been accepted because of this. It is not a character flaw, either you have it or you don't.

This constant testing and appraisal went on like this for about a week until finally it was time to face the music and find out whether I had it or not. I was called into the training staff office where one of the trainers sat me down and looked through my file. He started by saying that if there had not been a hard physical component to the selection week then I would probably have exploded with tension. Once my heart well and truly in my mouth, he informed me that I was deemed suitable for a training course. However, the commander would be seeing us the next day as there were about six of us who had made the grade for only four positions. What a great way to return the tension and stress levels right back up to maximum.

After a very sleepless night I attended the Dog Squad offices the next day and saw the commander. I walked in with a certain amount of confidence which was soon deflated. I was deeply disappointed when told that because at that time I lived in northern Sydney and those positions were full I would not be on the next course and would have to wait for the next one in about a year's time. What could I do? I copped it on the chin, thanked him and walked out. Another officer from the Central Coast received the same news so we travelled home via a hotel, both very disappointed.

Come Now or Never

About two weeks later, having just returned home at 6am after work, the phone rang. On the other end was the senior dog trainer for the squad. 'Do you still want to be in the Dog Squad? One of the other blokes has stress fractures in his leg so you can have his spot.' I was in a bit of a foggy daze but the words soon registered.

I answered, 'Of course I do but I've just finished work.'

'I want you to go to Menai now, pick up a vehicle, then get out here to Orchard Hills, but if you're too tired I'll get someone else.'

'I'm on my way.'

I wasn't tired anymore. I was excited into action. I went into the city and got one of the boys from the Transit Police to give me a lift to Menai. I did all he asked and got out to Orchard Hills which is a Defence Force establishment in western Sydney. It is basically made up of flat grass paddocks and areas of thick bushland.

I was sorry for the other guy but this was my opportunity. (The other officer involved is now an operational dog handler). Finally I had made it onto a training course, but not yet into the Dog Squad.

The Training Course

I f I thought I was going to see the three other guys in the same state that I had left them two weeks earlier then I was in for a rude shock. I walked into the meal room at Orchard Hills full of beans and enthusiasm. What I saw were three totally exhausted blokes who were barely able to raise a smile, definitely not the same guys who had been over the moon about getting on the course. Bloody hell, I thought, what's been going on here? Before I could ask, I was taken to the kennels to meet my dog, Training Dog Merlin.

He was at that time a twelve-month-old German shepherd with a classic black-and-tan coat. I also noticed that he was one of the biggest dogs I had ever seen, about 45kg at the time. As far as I was concerned, he was also the best looking dog I had ever seen. I was told by the senior trainer to 'Take him for a walk and make friends with him.' We walked for about a kilometre, and I watched everything he did intently. He was enjoying trotting along and stopping every now and again to have a sniff at the ground (we call this perving) then relieved himself. He looked at me a few times but probably thought I was just another bloke taking him for a walk. There was absolutely no bond with each other yet. We came to a big shady tree where I produced a rubber ring. Merlin immediately focused on this and started to wag his tail. I dropped down to his level and hid the ring under my stomach. He loved this and burrowed his nose into my curled up body in an attempt to retrieve the ring. This would turn out to be our favourite game, wrestling with each other like a couple of brothers in the backyard. He was barking and growling in a playful way and I didn't realise it yet but this was the start of our close bond which would make us the best of mates in years to come. We finished our wrestle and walked back. I was definitely on cloud nine. I was getting paid to work and play with dogs, and it didn't get much better than this. So far so good, I'd made it through the first hour and Merlin appeared to like me. I put him in the back of my police truck and was summonsed into the trainer's office.

I had a one-on-one with the head trainer. I was about to be slammed back to earth with the realisation that the hard work both mentally and physically was just about to start. He told me I'd already missed out on two weeks so I was behind the eight ball. 'The dog's good, so if you fail it won't be his fault, it's going to be yours. If you fall behind you will be left behind, permanently.'

I found out later from my course mates that the first two weeks had involved them being constantly screamed at and abused by the trainers. They had been quite literally run and exercised into the ground each and every day. Any mistake, whether it be not properly praising your dog to letting him relieve himself in the compound (a hanging offence) would usually mean a physical penalty for the course and a personal abuse session for the individual involved. One of the guys was brought to tears when told be was a reserve grader and not a first grader. This may seem a bit harsh by today's politically correct standards, but everybody was treated the same and the method was only to weed out those people who couldn't hack a bit of pressure. If you can't take a bit of abuse in a controlled environment, then how the hell are you going to face up to aggressive and violent offenders out on the street when it's just you and the dog? It's just my opinion but nothing beats a bit of good old-fashioned mental and physical toughness. The head trainer was one of those people who could make you drop your bundle by his mere presence. We ended up calling him Darth Vader because of the way he stalked around and made everybody nervous.

The second morning I arrived out at the training grounds and drove to a rear paddock where we were allowed to let our dogs relieve themselves. I got straight out and let Merlin go from the rear of the truck. He trotted out and started to do his business when suddenly he turned and shot off through the trees. I yelled out 'No' when I realised what he was doing. He had spotted a mob of kangaroos and was in the process of chasing them down. I looked around to see if anyone was watching. This was a bad thing and I knew if I was seen I was in trouble. I couldn't see anyone else so I ran out after Merlin who was fast becoming the centre of stress in my life. Finally, when he had had enough he came back. I couldn't get angry as he was now where I wanted him to be.

Just as I was putting him in the truck and congratulating myself on not getting caught, Vader came out from behind a tree and stood there staring at me with his clenched fists resting on his waist. He said, 'Do I have to say anything?'

I said, 'No, I won't let that happen again.' He told me that was good and that he was going to drive my truck back while I ran the 5km. This was to make sure that I remembered to keep Merlin on his lead the next morning. I was cursing and sweating all the way back to the compound and offices where I got out of my overalls, into my running gear and did the daily 5km run with my course mates.

One morning I had laid a track down for one of my course mates. I had walked three legs putting an article half way along the first two then at the end of the last so that the dog would get his reward. This meant that I had walked in a straight line for about 100m then changed direction and walked another 100m in a straight line then again for a third time. On each of these 100m legs I would put down a small article which is a toy reward for the dog to play with as he tracked up to each one. This teaches the dog that when he follows human scent he receives a reward each time. At the end of the third leg he would receive another article and have a huge play with his handler as a reward. Eventually the tracks would be four legs up to an hour old with the entire length about a kilometre.

Vader was running late that day so my mate wanted to get his track done before he arrived. This course mate was at the time doing very well and tracking with a lot of confidence. He sat his dog at the start of the track and unravelled his tracking line. Just then, Vader's four-wheel drive appeared at the edge of the paddock making a beeline for us. He wasn't even out of his car when our mate started to rush. He put on his dog's tracking harness back to front and dropped his tracking line. All the time he was looking back at Vader who just stood there and stared. He didn't say a word as my course mate's track went out the door. I'll just say that this track turned out to be one of his worst and cost him many, many penalty kilometres.

I was not immune to this either. One morning I was harnessing Merlin up for the same kind of track. We had done a few good ones in a row so I was full of confidence. I had left Merlin sitting in front of the track's start, taken off his lead and turned to pick up his tracking harness when without my knowledge he took off tracking unharnessed. I turned back to find there was no dog to put the harness on. He was 20m away and tracking. I yelled out for him to come back but he kept on going until he picked up the first article. He held it in his mouth then taunted me by prancing back and forth moving further away each time I tried to get close and put him on his lead. 'Come here, you little smart arse' was about all I could come up with at the time. Just like a child, he seemed to know which buttons to push and how far he dare push them before I would explode. Again he came back when he was done. It was early days and he did not yet see me as the leader of the pack.

One track did go well in the early stages of the course. I had finished playing with Merlin to reward him and was walking back to Vader who was standing with the other trainers to receive my debrief. Vader turned to me and said, 'You finally did it right, it's about time. Don't think I'm going to give you a pat on the back. Go back and wait for us.' That was about as close to a compliment as I was ever going to get from him.

The exercising type of torture was not the only kind we had to deal with during the course. After each and every exercise we would have to play with the dogs to give them a reward. No matter how tired we were, the 'play' had to be vibrant and exciting for the dog. It would be done with a favourite toy (Merlin's was the rubber ring) building up to a peak then stopping while the dog was most excited. These 'plays' would result in numerous and constant bites to the hands and body, leaving especially the hands very sore all the time. No matter how much it hurt, you could not show any anger towards the dog, only happy praise as the bites were accidental and only inflicted because he was very excited. I got one beauty on the back just under my armpit. If you reach around and give yourself a pinch there you will see how sensitive that area is. Merlin put a K-9 into it when he missed an article I was holding in front of him. I stupidly turned in an effort to hide the article and paid a very painful price. I had a scar from that for about two years before it went away.

This was the kind of mental and physical torture which went on for about three months. If you can survive this and come out the other end, then you have really achieved something worth being proud of. Out of the four of us that eventually went on the course, three of us came through. One of the guys started to come up with excuses every morning, complaining of injuries that prevented him from running. He would however be able to jump around and do everything else for the rest of the day. This was not lost on the three of us or the trainers who eventually put him out of his misery and sent him home.

The training course is designed to teach us as novice handlers and to train the dogs to a novice standard. There are five basic exercises that need to be successfully completed:

1. OBEDIENCE/HEEL WORK. This is pretty self explanatory. If you don't have a basic control over the dog then there is no way you are going to be able to conduct the harder exercises later on. It also highlights the fact that the dog has no respect for you. The excercise includes having the dog walk and run at the heel position, which is at the handler's left side. Obedience also involves a number of different commands that enable you to put your dog in a controlled position. All have to be able to be given by both voice and hand signals.

2. AGILITY. This exercise is to give the dog self-confidence when confronted by obstacles. There are a number of obstacles used in training. They include a ladder and plank climb, hurdles that are about a metre high, a broad jump, tunnel and high wall scale which is about 2m high. Initially, all these exercises are done with an article (a toy which the dog likes) to help increase the enjoyment level for the dog. All the heights start out low so that they are always successful and all exercises are done with a high level of enthusiasm from the handlers. If you're not enthusiastic and animated, this is directly transferred to the dog's performance. In other words, if he does poorly then you get the kick up the arse. Out on the street you can't have your dog stopping and hesitating while you're hunting down an offender. He has to be able to keep going no matter what's in the way.

3. TRACKING. This is the bread and butter of the Police Dog Team. If your dog can't track, then he can't become a police dog. This is the most effective means of catching offenders who have fled a crime scene. There are a number of categories involved with tracking. First is grass tracking. This is where the dog is first taught how to follow a human scent on the ground. Soft grass surfaces are the best to start teaching the dog to track on. The second is hard surface tracking which involves anything from dirt surfaces to concrete and bitumen. This is harder for the dog and is usually done at a slower pace. He and the handler have to concentrate much harder. The third is the culmination of the first two and is called operational tracking that involves tracking in the real world over all types of surfaces and obstacles. The first two are conducted in sterile areas where there is no other scent other than the human one that is being followed. Operational tracking has all the other scents and smells found in the real world. You have to watch the dog very carefully. Training Merlin and myself to learn this art was the hardest thing I have ever done. There are many and varied skills which have to be learnt and mastered. I will not go into them now as I could literally go on for about a hundred pages But one of the training tracks early on in the course ended up with me being put in Merlin's tracking harness and being made to crawl the 200m back to our car, all the time having the tracking line which is attached to the harness pulled and jerked making it very hard work. To make it even more fun, the trainer on the other end was shouting 'How do you like it? You must not jerk the line, it must be kept at a constant tension.'

After this I always worked on getting it right. It was a really effective way of learning the lesson.

4. SEARCHING. This is pretty self-explanatory. Our dogs are taught to run out away from us and search outside areas including bushland and school grounds. This is called an Open Search. The second is a Building Search and quite obviously is where the dog searches a building. The dog will signal the handler that he has found someone and will stay with them. They are not taught to bite the people on searches as they are not always criminals we are looking for. It could be a child lost in the bush. The only people who get bitten in these situations are those who decide to try and shut the dog up. This usually entails some kind of violent act, which generally means the dog will take hold of the offender until the handler arrives and orders him off. I still can't work out why offenders do that. I mean if someone points a gun at you, you can call their bluff but if a police dog has you cornered, there's no bluff. If you take him on then you're usually going to get hurt. Searching is the quickest and easiest way to clear a large area or building that would take police officers ten times as long.

5. MAN WORK. This is where the dog is taught to chase down and bite an offender. He also learns a 'Call Off' which allows a handler to stop the attack if the offender for example drops his weapon and stops running. These skills are tested on a regular basis. He is also taught handler protection, which means that if anybody comes too close or attacks me, the dog is going to take him or her out. Police dogs are taught to bite hard and hold on until told to stop by the handler. These skills take a long time to teach. The methods and commands used are a reasonably well-kept secret for obvious reasons. Contrary to popular belief, police dogs are not psychotic killers. We don't want dogs that will kill everything in their way. Our dogs have a controlled aggression. They will bite only when necessary or when told to do so.

I have given a basic overall view of the types of skills that a General Purpose Police Dog and handler must master before graduating as an operational team. If I were to go into detail about how we achieve the outcomes for each exercise you would become very bored and I would be writing for the next ten years. Again I have to say, this course took about four months and was the hardest thing I have ever attempted. It is the most physically and mentally draining course I have ever done. The thing that kept me going at the times where it would have been easier to give up was that if this was easy, then anybody could do it. The fact is that I hate to lose, and failure to complete this course would personally have been a huge loss. Out of the four of us, three made the grade as police dog handlers. One was returned to his previous duties. A good bloke but he didn't quite have what it took to complete the course. You have to have a certain amount of toughness to put up with the constant pressure put on you by the trainers, because you want to achieve the best results for the dog and yourself.

Of the seven dogs who started the course, three were sacked as unsuitable. All three were unable to track to an acceptable level. As a general rule, only about three out of every hundred dogs looked at by the Dog Squad make the grade as police dogs.

There are a number of characteristics the Dog Squad looks for when selecting a dog for training. First, they must have a strong impulse to retrieve and they need to show a strong desire and willingness to find and retrieve objects. They have to have a strong desire to play because all rewards for a police dog are through voice praise and play. If they don't have a play then how are they to be rewarded for doing the exercises? All the exercises are basically done the same way every time.

The dog knows, for example, if I put on his tracking harness then he has to put his nose down and track automatically.

We don't reward with food. The dog needs to be confident. Some situations require the dog to search buildings in pitch black away from the handler. If he's not sure of himself then he won't stay with the offender and most likely won't find him in the first place. The dogs have to be physically fit, with no defects. The dog must be alert to what's going on around him and cannot be hand shy—simply raising your hand at the dog while he's in front of you completes this test. If he shies away then it's probably a good bet that someone has physically abused him. Because we get a lot of donated dogs this is one of the first things we check. We cannot have a dog run and hide when a violent offender starts kicking and punching at the dog or handler.

Another trait is to see how inquisitive the dog is. When going to see a dog, I go to the side fence and look over. If the dog races up and barks then he's probably unsure and scared. If he comes up and looks at you, that shows he just wants to check you out and see what you're up to. Merlin has ambushed a few people in my yard this way. They've come down the side gate and been confronted by him after he's stalked them under the house. Most of the time they never heard or saw him, just the way I like it. Just like good police officers, the dog needs to be methodical and check everything. The ideal age for training is between twelve months and two years. This is not a hard and fast rule as there have been older dogs trained and some training can be done with younger dogs.

One of the most important things with a working dog is to develop a bond with them. Just like with human relationships, some people get on with certain people and not others. It is the same with dogs and their handlers, although it might take longer with some dogs and a shorter time with others. If a dog has a good strong bond with you then he is going to work for you all the time even when the going gets tough. To really bond with a dog you need to spend time with him. That is why Merlin comes home with me and is part of the family. Home is a place for him to relax and recharge his batteries. Just like us he needs to have down time from the stresses of work.

Because of the great and even temperament that all successful police dogs have, home life is pretty straight forward. Merlin is great with kids and the rest of my family but because he is a pack animal he needs to realise that he is at the bottom of the pack and that all other family members are above him. Even though he has a great temperament I never leave him out of sight with anyone—you never know when he might decide to climb a rung on the ladder. I also had to teach members of the family about basic dog mentality and how to act around Merlin when he was out of his kennel at home. I made it clear they are never to try and give him any commands—he must listen to me and me alone. Sticking to some basic rules has meant that I have never had any problems with him at home and he is a much loved member of the family.

One funny incident was a training exercise on a very quiet railway station platform in the inner city when we were away from Orchard Hills and introducing the dogs to the real world. It was about 9pm on a weekday. One of the trainers was dressed in a very ratty tracksuit with a very smelly and long wig on his head. We had to walk along the platform. He was going to jump up from a seat and threaten the dog and handler. This exercise was to create suspicion for the dog. Finally the trainer would assault us and we would allow the dog to attack (the trainer was wearing a concealed attack arm). Each handler went through the exercise. During the last one we heard a number of sirens but thought nothing of it. Suddenly six officers from Redfern

Police came bounding up the stairs and came to a sudden halt. 'We had a report of people setting their dogs on a bloke and robbing him.' If the person who reported this had had a closer look he or she would have seen that we were wearing police overalls with 'POLICE' written in large lettering on the back! We used the Redfern boys as an angry group for training the dogs and chased them off the platform. The dogs don't see in colour and don't know the difference between police and members of the community.

The last hurdle was the accreditation (testing) of the handler and dog as a team, including a written test. I didn't do very well on the written test—I have never been good at them—so by the time I got to the practical testing, I was very nervous and knew I would have to do well for an overall pass. I was nervous as hell and had a short and sincere chat to Merlin before we attempted each exercise. Trainers and senior staff members who had not been part of the training course did the marking. Thankfully, he's a great dog who didn't realise the pressure was on and performed very well even if I was rather highly strung through the whole process.

The day finally came when I went into the Commander's office. He leaned over his desk, shook my hand and told me that I had been successful then welcomed me into the squad. I was now a very novice handler. 'The standards are high and you will be expected to live up to those standards. Well done,' he said. I walked out on top of the world. Finally I had made it in. Now the real work was about to begin and we were going out into the real world.

Buddy Time

The first four weeks out on the road is spent with an experienced dog handler who is your 'buddy'. It's his job to get you acquainted with the job. My buddy was from the Central Coast of NSW. I'll call him by his nickname, Spud. Spud is a very experienced police dog handler and trainer. He's also a top bloke. I'd drive up to Gosford Police Station at the start of my shift and meet him.

On the second day, which started at 4.30pm, we were driving around when a call came over the police radio with a description of an escapee who had bolted from one of the city courts the day before. This person was also believed to be armed with a firearm. Spud added to this by telling me that this criminal had been seen on the Central Coast driving around in a green Tarago van. I took in the information then put it to the back of my mind, as I really didn't expect to see either the van or the crook. I'm not that lucky. Just before sunset Spud and I drove to Green Point. I didn't know the Central Coast that well so I was happy to follow directions. Then it happened. I saw the green Tarago driving towards us. I checked the number plate and saw that there was only one person on board. It was the same van that Spud had told me about. I couldn't believe my luck! I turned to Spud and said, 'That's the bloody van with the escapee.'

I pulled on the handbrake and performed a screeching U-turn. The van pulled to the side of the road and the driver got out and ran into the bush. All I saw was a male wearing a hooded jumper and carrying something in his left hand. I pulled up and ran to the rear of the police car. I was in the process of opening the tailgate when Spud asked me what I was going to do. I told him that I was going to release Merlin from the back of the car to search for the offender. He was only about ten seconds ahead of us and I knew that Merlin could easily run him down. Spud said, 'No, no, no, you should track him.' Being new I had no choice but to agree.

I harnessed Merlin into his tracking gear, which includes a leather harness and about thirty feet of lead. Spud asked for my portable radio. He told me his was not working. He also told me that he would inform police radio of what was occurring. I just agreed and started to track. Merlin almost ripped off my arms when we started. We tracked into thick grass where he located a baseball bat that the offender had dropped. We continued on to a dirt trail that led behind a row of houses. One lady called out and told me, 'He's running towards the creek.' This was the way that we were tracking. All I could think of was the fact that it was only the second day and we were going to get an armed escapee, you beauty!

The track continued down into a thick wood and scrub area beside a creek. By this time it was becoming quite dark and very hard to see. Merlin who had been absolutely powering along (as this was a 'hot track' which means it was less than five minutes old) came to a stop and started to look around. I knew that the offender was very close. All of a sudden Merlin started to growl. He darted under a low bush. I heard a scream. 'He's got him,' I shouted then started to draw my firearm, fearing that the offender might still be armed. Spud grabbed my hand from behind and said, 'No, don't worry your dog's got him.'

I said, 'I'm not taking the chance.'

Spud became quite insistent and told me to forget the gun and go under the bush. So I did. I saw Merlin with his jaws around the offender's right arm. The offender still had on the hood and was screaming. He tried to get up so I pushed him down and he stayed down. I was then able to call off Merlin. Just after having done this and thinking you bloody beauty I've caught a crook on only my second day, the offender looked up, smiled and held out his left hand as if to shake mine. I was about to tell him to piss off when I heard Spud say, 'Matt, say hello to Tony, he's from the Dog Squad.'

It took about thirty seconds for it all to sink into my head. Those bastards. Tony set me up. I think the pair of them was laughing at the look on my face rather than the fact that their plan had worked to perfection. I had been totally deceived. I thought it was real and all the pieces finally fitted in. Spud telling me all afternoon about the escapee and his van, making us track, taking the radio and stopping me from drawing my firearm. It took me about an hour to calm down. On the other hand, it was the best kind of training because I thought it was real. Bastards.

First Catch

This was a pretty important day for the two of us. We were finally out on our own and patrolling around the Sydney Metropolitan area on a weeknight. At about 11pm we were called down to a cement factory in Pyrmont along the waterfront. The compound was about 100x200m. There were about twenty cement trucks parked inside and 200m-high silos at the rear along the waterfront which formed the rear perimeter. There were also a number of demountable buildings which were the office areas.

The police already at the scene told me that two males with backpacks on had been seen climbing through the fence but had not come out. The walls to either side of the compound were about 5m high with barbed wire on top, so they had to be in there. You beauty, here we come. I got Merlin out and made for the hole left in the fence. I got him geed up by making him bark and gave a warning in a loud voice, 'Police, come out or I'll send the dog.' I gave him a command for searching (I'm not going to make it generally known what our commands are) and he darted off into the compound. I waited for about five minutes at the hole as I could hear Merlin panting and moving around in the dark, occasionally knocking things over. He kept going back to the base of the stairs, which ran up the side of one of the silos and looked up.

Okay, I thought, nothing is ever easy. The most logical place for the intruders to go is up. It's the hardest place for the dog to find them. After a quick look around the compound to make sure that Merlin hadn't missed them, I started to climb the stairs with him on his lead. The stairs were a metal grate, which meant that you could see straight down through them. This was fine for me but the big fella wasn't so sure. For dogs, this is very disconcerting. We were going higher and the ground was getting further away from him however he did very well. I encouraged him up and he would occasionally lift his head up towards the top of the silo and growl. At the time there was quite a strong breeze blowing and I knew that Merlin was smelling somebody up there. This was starting to get the adrenalin flowing in me. What if the intruders at the top wanted to fight when we got there? It's 100m down. Oh well, we'll just have to find out when we get there. Finally we made it to the top. The silo we were on had a concrete cover and nothing else. No rail along the side, nothing. However there was a metal ladder, which led to the next silo, which was about 10m higher. As soon as we walked towards the ladder Merlin started to bark in the direction of the next silo. He was quite literally trying to pull me over the edge towards it. I had to use a lot of strength to stop him, but I knew one hundred per cent that the offenders were up there.

I yelled out repeatedly for them to come down. The police at the bottom of the silo could hear me. Eventually I came to the conclusion that the only way to get them down was for someone to go and get them. We couldn't as there was no way Merlin was going to be able to climb the ladder. Eventually two police came up and crossed over to the other silo. About ten seconds later I heard them ordering someone to come out. Soon after, two males were sent down the ladder to be greeted by a barking and snarling Merlin. 'Is he going to bite me?' asked one of them. 'Only if you misbehave or fight us,' was my reply.

Needless to say they both behaved and were very polite from then on. The police who had come up to help told me that the two offenders had been hiding in a small cupboard on the other side of the second silo. I was very happy with the result and it just goes to show how good a sense of smell a dog has.

The two intruders were charged with Break and Enter and Entering Enclosed Lands (trespassing). Not the crime of the century but I was relieved to have made our first arrest as a team.

First Violent Offender

It was only a week or so after our first catch that I drove into the Dog Squad base at Menai at about 9am. I spoke to our operations co-ordinator who asked me to go down the road with a couple of detectives who wanted to arrest a male who had warrants out for his arrest. He was going to be sent straight to gaol without passing go. The address was inside a housing commission complex only 300m away. I spoke to the detectives who told me that they had tried on three other occasions to arrest this guy but he had run and evaded them on each occasion. This is where the dog comes into play. You can run but you can't hide. This sounded easy and was probably a good chance for Merlin to search for an offender.

We travelled down and parked around a corner from the complex then walked in. The detectives walked to the front door while I stayed down the side of the townhouse with a view of the front and rear. Amazingly, the criminal we were after answered the door and was immediately grabbed, handcuffed and placed under arrest. Too easy. He started to cry and plead with his girlfriend to do something.

Too bad mate, if you can't do the time, then don't do the crime. I walked with them back to our vehicles and started to put Merlin away when this offender pushed one of the detectives to the ground and started to run, even though he was still handcuffed to his front. He ran straight back into the townhouse complex.

I grabbed Merlin's lead and we were off after him. I called on him to stop a number of times but he just kept on running. I tell you what, he was running bloody fast for a guy who was handcuffed. I guess the thought of going to prison was having the effect of half a kilo of steroids. He reached a fence at the rear of the complex which led into a paddock then onto a main road. I let go of Merlin's lead and gave a command. He raced ahead and took hold of the offender's right leg just as he was going over the fence. I grabbed his jumper and pulled him back to our side. He fell right on top of me and immediately started to try and drive the handcuffs into my face. He got a couple of good shots on me until I managed to grab his arms and turn him onto his side. He kept on trying to smash my face with the handcuffs but suddenly went limp then started to scream in pain. I was at a loss until I remembered Merlin.

'Good boy,' I shouted when I looked down at the offender's legs. I saw that my best mate was not going to put up with this violent maniac having a go at his dad. Merlin had the criminals right knee in his jaws with the front upper canines embedded all the way into his kneecap. I stood up and gave a command. Merlin let go and came back to my side and on to his lead. I gave him a pat on the head and another 'good boy' as the detectives picked up the now sobbing offender and dragged him off to gaol. Merlin trotted back to the car with his chest puffed up, letting everyone know that he was the biggest and baddest man on the street. He had taken on his first violent human offender and won, big time.

I was very happy and proud because I now knew that Merlin was going to look after me in the real world. This gave me a lot of confidence especially when facing bigger, more violent and armed offenders in the future.

Always Write It Down

This job started at one end of Sydney and ended on the other. It was about 4pm on a Monday afternoon and I was just starting work. I heard a call over the police radio channel in northern Sydney for police to keep a look out for a stolen white Laser hatchback. They gave the registration number, which I wrote on my hand just in case. The occupants of this vehicle had just committed an armed robbery at Lane Cove using a blood-filled syringe. This form of weapon is a very frightening prospect for the victims with the thought of being stabbed and infected with HIV a very real possibility.

About an hour later I was in Parramatta Police Station, which lies in the western suburbs of Sydney. I heard a call from one of the local cars, 'Parramatta 300 Urgent, I'm on Park Street, Harris Park. Two males have run from a white Laser after a smash. I'm in foot pursuit.' He gave the registration number of the Laser. I looked at my hand and, yes, it was the same one. I got on my radio and told them why the offenders were running. Not long after, the Parramatta officer lost the two armed robbers in a back street that had a large building site on it. I arrived a short time later with about twenty other police who had set up a large perimeter around the block.

I went back to where the officer had last seen them then put Merlin into his tracking harness. We tracked down into a side street then over a backyard fence into the rear yard of a house that was right next to the building site in the centre of the block. Unfortunately, to go over the fence would have been difficult for Merlin as there were ditches and a lot of debris on the other side. However, I could see a set of fresh footprints in the mud. We had a very good perimeter set in place so I reasoned that the chances of at least one of the robbers being in there were pretty good.

We ran back around to the entrance, climbing through a small hole in the wire fence. Inside was a six-storey half-built apartment block with scaffolding all around. On the opposite side was a huge pile of stacked bricks about 2m high. I gave the challenge of, 'Police, come out or I'll send the dog.' I gave a now barking Merlin a command and let him off his lead. He ran straight out into the centre of the site then started to search along the perimeter. When he went past the stack of bricks he started to hackle up, his tail went straight into the air and he lifted his nose towards the top of the brick pile. I shouted, 'Good boy'. I knew he'd found someone. Merlin started to jump up the side of the brick pile so he could locate and bark at the offender. He was almost there when up jumped a very nervous armed robber who shouted, 'Okay, keep that thing away from me.' As he came to the edge, Merlin made it up and started to run at him. Before I could call the big fella off, the big, tough armed robber jumped off the pile of bricks about 2m to the ground and ran to the nearest officer and hid behind him. He was handcuffed and taken away. When I stopped laughing along with the rest of the police, we searched for the other offender who had unfortunately escaped the perimeter. Still, one armed robber is better than none.

Free Lunch

As a police dog team we spend a lot of time walking the street in industrial, residential and commercial areas. It's a lot easier to see what's going on when you're walking as opposed to driving around. It was about midday on a beautiful spring day in Sydney and we found ourselves walking the beat around the Corso in Manly. This area is blocked off to traffic and there are numerous shops, restaurants, cafés and pubs in the area, with Manly beach at its easternmost end.

Merlin was quite happily walking at my side as we approached a café, which has outdoor tables along the footpath. I wasn't paying attention to what he was doing—I was watching a group of drunken pommies who had just stumbled out of one of the more infamous pubs in the area.

A businessman sitting at an outside table had a chicken and avocado sandwich in his hand and as we walked past him. Without missing a beat, Merlin snatched it out of his hand and swallowed it in one motion. I just caught sight of it disappearing down his big, greedy throat. I turned to the businessman and was lost for words. He just kept looking at his hand and at Merlin. His mate was doubled over with laughter and had turned the colour of a beetroot he was laughing so hard. I said I was very sorry and that I'd pay for a new sandwich. Luckily for me he had a good sense of humour and started to laugh along with his mate. He said, 'No, don't worry, this is going to be a great story to tell at work and the pub, mate.' I asked him a few more times to let me pay for the sandwich but he wouldn't take the money. I was still bloody embarrassed when we parted company. It just goes to show that even with all their training and discipline, dogs are dogs and I should have seen it coming. We don't walk near diners anymore.

Tug Of War

We were enjoying a reasonably busy Wednesday night in Sydney's northern beaches area. We had rushed around to a couple of jobs and although we hadn't been able to make any catches it was good to be busy and not sitting around waiting for something to happen. We had just finished up a foot patrol of the industrial area of Allambie Heights when out of the blue there was a sudden rise in my adrenaline levels.

'Hornsby 35 urgent, we're in pursuit.' I turned up the volume level and gunned it out of the driveway, switching on the lights and sirens to clear the way. We were about 15–20km from the pursuit and I had to get there as fast as possible in case the driver jumped out and legged it. Luckily for me, the pursuit went on for about ten minutes. The Hornsby car was chasing a stolen van which had just been involved in a break and enter. The driver of the van was trying to evade the pursuing police car in back streets as there was no way he was going to be able to outrun them on a main road. Another lucky point was that it was about 11.30pm and the backstreets of Hornsby were deserted—there were no children playing outside which greatly reduced the danger levels and the chance of a tragedy. Eventually, with three police cars chasing, the desperate thief made a mistake and backed himself into a corner. He turned down a dead-end street which led into a bush gully that was 500x500m in area. It had houses all around and ran up a steep hill on one side. He locked up the van tyres which skidded up over the gutter and onto dirt where he came to a stop. The driver jumped out while the van was still moving and sprinted into the gully, quickly disappearing from sight. He was dressed all in black and was carrying a black backpack.

The pursuing police did everything right. They knew I was on the way and not far off. They sent police to all sides of the gully, trapping him inside. I arrived soon after knowing we had a really good chance of catching this thieving lunatic. I stood at the edge of the bush with Merlin and I yelled out as loud as I could, 'Police, come out now or I'm sending in the dog.' I got no reply. I yelled out the same again, noticing that my words were echoing off the trees and steep terrain. Still no reply. Merlin was doing his part by barking and champing at the bit to get going. The low-level bushes and vine-covered trees were going to make tracking with a long tracking line near impossible as we would definitely get caught up and bogged down. I gave the crook one more chance to surrender yelling at the top of my voice while Merlin assisted with his deep, excited bark. Nothing.

I gave Merlin his command and he steamed off into the bush vaulting a fallen tree and running out of sight. I started in and fell over about three times as there were holes and rotten wood all over the ground. I could hear Merlin working with his nose and crashing through the same undergrowth with a lot more ease than me. Of course the crook wasn't going to make it easy for me. I could hear Merlin working his way up the steep hill as he honed in on the crook's scent. I did my best but was falling behind and wished that I had a machete to help fight my way through the vines and prickly lantana bushes. Eventually I made my way out onto a small clearing just in time to see Merlin scramble up a retaining wall at the bottom of someone's property. He was wagging his tail and giving his low growl. This guy was near. Two seconds later I heard Merlin start to bark in excitement telling me that he had found the runner. Not long after that the barking stopped being replaced with a growl. I could hear a man's voice pleading, 'No, no, give it back.' I went up the same retaining wall and when I lit up the area with my torch I saw Merlin engaged in a tug of war with the thief and his black backpack. Merlin had hold of the bag in his jaws with the crook holding on for dear life with both hands. He was on his backside being dragged down the hill towards me. I yelled out, 'Good boy' and forced the crook onto his chest. This broke his hold on the bag.

He was sobbing and crying like a little baby. I could see that he was covered in gaol tattoos but was not acting as tough as his tattoos would suggest he should. He whined at me that he didn't want to go back to gaol and that he was on parole. In fact it turns out that this was his *first* day out of gaol! He had decided that instead of enjoying the opportunities of freedom the right way he would go on a crime spree. I said he should have thought of that before he made his decision, and that he had no one to blame but himself. To make it even worse for him, the bag he had fought Merlin over had thirty separate plastic bags of amphetamine deals inside. So not only was he going to be charged with break and enter, stealing a car, running from the police in a pursuit, a van full of stolen property and breaching his parole, he was going to face supply of illegal drug charges as well. All within the twelve hours of being released from prison. Maybe he'll be able to control himself next time he gets released.

Learn From Your Mistakes

After about three months on the road we had had a few successes and perhaps I had become a little overconfident in our ability. My overconfidence was about to have the stuffing punched out of it. It was about 3pm on a summer day and I was starting to think about heading home. I was up near Hornsby in northern Sydney when a call came over the police radio for a dog to go to channel H, which covers Carlingford to Merrylands. I switched over and found that I was the only dog available and that the job was only about five minutes away at Telopea. There was a gaol escapee who had gone to ground in a residential area. There was a huge number of police on a perimeter including General Duties, Detectives and Polair (Police helicopter).

I arrived in a blaze of glory and spoke to the police who had chased him on foot. They showed me to a driveway at a house and said that he had run up there then they had lost sight of him. They had done all the right things as far as the Dog Squad is concerned. They had not gone into the area so that the human scent left by the escapee was not contaminated, and they had organised a perimeter quickly. I got Merlin and harnessed him into his tracking gear. He put his nose to the ground and tracked up the driveway. It went to a back fence and stopped. This should have told me something but I chose to ignore the fact that if the track stops like that then he has probably gone to ground and is hiding nearby. Instead I was convinced that he had jumped fences and was further up hiding in another yard somewhere. I took Merlin out of his tracking harness and sent him out to search. This was the second mistake as I failed to read his body language. He ran out all right and started to search but after a short time was slowing down and was not very interested in searching. This was a good indication that the offender had not come this way, as there was no scent to keep Merlin interested. But, like the boofhead that I am, I pushed him on until we reached the railway line. By this time I had numerous detectives and Polair following me. I harnessed him up again and found a track, which led to a hole in the fence on the rail line. He was tracking again and I was convinced that he had gone this way. I had this huge police circus following Merlin and myself. We tracked up to a backyard fence where I heard voices on the other side. I looked over and saw four blokes having a barbecue. I asked them whether they had seen anyone walking the line and whether they had seen anyone jump their fence recently. They told me that all four of them had just walked the way I tracked, as it was a shortcut from the bottle shop to the house.

Just as I received this information, a call came over the police radio. 'Rosehill 15 urgent. The offender had just run out from under the house where the dog started. We're in foot pursuit.' Then about ten seconds later they called that they had the offender in custody. I then received a call from police radio, 'Dog 545 did you copy that?' I could sense the tone in that voice. I looked back to the group of detectives who had simply turned and started to walk back to the initial scene without saying a word. I turned and walked back. To make matters worse, I had to walk back along the street where all the residents were standing out the front of their houses watching me. They had all seen me arrive and search their street. They had all seen the escapee run

LEARN FROM YOUR MISTAKES

after I had left and been caught by the General Duties Police. I got all the smart arse remarks and sniggers as I walked back to my car. I felt like a moron and wanted to just curl up in a ball and die. It was my fault, not Merlin's or anybody else's. I was the one who didn't read him properly and I was the one who pushed on thinking I knew best. Yes, I was glad that the escapee had been caught but it was a real lesson in humility. I just climbed into the car and skulked away.

In some ways it was good as I made some huge mistakes but learnt some very good lessons from them. It's good to learn from your mistakes but geez I wish my mistakes hadn't been so very public.

Cabramatta

C abramatta was a bit of a political football but like all the police who work in this area I don't have anything to do with all the high-level finger pointing and mud slinging. Myself and other dog teams were tasked to go out there to support the local police and maintain a high visibility presence. There are a lot of hard working and honest people who live and work in this suburb. These people are in the unfortunate position of having to put up with a concentration of drug dealers and the addicts whom they attract. When I first started to work this area even I was astounded by the sheer scale of the drug problem out there. I thought Kings Cross was bad but that place paled into insignificance by comparison. It would be naive to think that the problems out there have now stopped but I can say that the dealers and users have been well and truly attacked and put into place by the police. I was involved in a great number of incidents in the Cabramatta area but there were a few which stood out.

It was only the second time that we had visited Cabramatta. I was walking with Merlin down one of the main streets at 8pm on a Friday. I was still getting a feel for the place. I was looking for places where junkies go to shoot up and or buy heroin. Most of these people regularly go back to the same places all the time. A large pile of syringes is usually a good place to start. I just happened to glance to my left as

I was walking past a block of units. I just saw the outline of a person squatting down in front of a garage door. Hello, I thought, what's this person up to? I started to walk towards him. Merlin saw him too and started to growl. I lit him up with my torch and saw a junkie at work with a needle in his arm, which was covered in his blood. I shouted out, 'Police, drop that needle and stay where you are!' The man promptly removed the syringe from his arm and started to walk towards us. To make the situation even more interesting, he had the sharp end of the syringe pointed out towards me in his right hand. He looked like he was performing a bayonet charge over no man's land.

I screamed at him this time to drop the syringe and stop walking. Merlin was going ballistic and telling him in his own special way that it probably wasn't such a good idea to keep coming at us. This junkie said, 'No, you don't understand' and kept on coming in the same way. Well, bugger this, I thought. I let him have it. He was about 1.5m from us when I released Merlin who jumped out and took hold of the junkie's right leg. At the same time I hit him as hard as I could across his right wrist with my torch, which thankfully made him drop the syringe. Not wanting to touch his bloodied arm or get into a wrestle with him, which may have also brought me into contact with his blood, we had a further short but violent struggle which sent the crook to the ground. When these type of altercations happen, you try to use what you learned at the Academy but, when you're faced with the prospect of having a dirty blood-filled syringe jabbed into you then any method to stop him quickly and effectively must be used. All the time, my big hairy mate had a hold of his leg which left a few large puncture holes in the offender. I called Merlin off and had him sit near the bad guy's head. Meanwhile I called for assistance from the local police who arrived and took him back to Cabramatta Police Station. I charged him with Assaulting Police. Much to my satisfaction he was sentenced to twelve months gaol after pleading guilty. I'm employed by the people of this state to stop these criminals and bring them to justice, preferably without violence, but sometimes they don't leave us any choice. The greatest weapon we have as police is the ability to communicate and resolve without physical confrontation. Sometimes though, like I said they leave us no other choice.

I was quite proud of Merlin in this next incident. It was an arrest in which we received a Deputy Commissioner's Commendation for bravery. It was about 4.30pm on a summer's day. I was in Cabramatta Police Station finishing up an earlier arrest and thinking about going home when I heard a call on the police radio regarding an armed robbery in progress at a real estate agency in Canley Vale. This is a suburb next to Cabramatta. A few seconds later, a Highway Patrol officer called a foot pursuit with the thief who he saw leaving the agency with a gun in his hand. I bolted out and screamed up there in the car. Luckily there were many other police on the road and the area was surrounded. The Highway Patrol officer had lost sight of the robber in a laneway at the rear of a row of shops on Canley Vale Road. A perimeter was set up and I arrived a few minutes later.

I put Merlin into his tracking harness and cast him across the laneway. The offender had been seen in this area only about two minutes beforehand. He put his nose on the ground and started to track very hard. I knew the offender wasn't far off so my heart was pumping and the adrenalin was flowing. I had an officer either side of me wearing ballistic vests and their guns drawn. We came to a fence about 10m down the laneway where Merlin stopped and indicated to me that someone had recently gone over. I had a quick look through a crack in the palings and saw nothing except a small grass yard with an old-fashioned outdoor toilet in it. The whole area was only about 3x5m. I told the two officers with me to cover us while we climbed the fence. So far, so good. The two police came over as well. Merlin was dragging me towards the free-standing outside toilet. I knew this robber was in there. We came up to the side then round to the front door that was shut. Merlin was starting to growl and I knew we had him. Just to be certain I sent one of the officers to see the staff of the shop to make sure it wasn't one of them in there. It wasn't. There was only one thing for it. I shouted out, 'Police, throw out your weapon and come out.' There was no response. I shouted the same thing again. Still nothing. I shouted it out for a third time and included a hard kick to the door, which only opened about 5cm then closed again. I didn't realise it at the time but the robber had been looking through a crack in the door and had his face up against it. The kick to the door opened him up to the tune of fourteen stitches to his forehead. I kicked and kicked but couldn't get the door to open or make the robber talk to me. By this time there were about ten police surrounding the toilet all with their weapons drawn and pointed at it.

The next moment I heard loud bangs from inside the toilet and dust started coming from the roof area. He wasn't shooting but at the time we couldn't work out what was happening. I gave the door one big kick and it flew open. I could see the armed robber with a gold chrome pistol in his hand standing on the toilet bowl. At the time it was pointed up at the ceiling. I later learned from him that he was trying to hide it in the roof, but, at the time all I knew was that he was armed and standing directly in front of me. I was in just about the worst place I could be, in the open with nowhere to hide if he decided to shoot. I let a now salivating and barking Merlin go. He jumped in and grabbed the armed robber's right leg. The crook started to punch Merlin to his head. BIG MISTAKE. Merlin let go and immediately bit the armed robber in his groin area. He took both testicles and penis then started to drag him out. There are no words to describe the screaming and crying coming from this person's mouth. You really had to be there and experience it. Merlin dragged him out and along the ground for about 2m. As one, all the police who were standing in the yard let out a collective 'Oooooooohhhhh' with a certain inspector adding, 'That's got to hurt.' I called off Merlin who came to my side. The robber rolled onto his stomach and looked like he was reaching for something in his jacket. I couldn't see the gun so I sent Merlin back. He grabbed him by his thigh and started to shake him like a rag doll. I screamed at him to show his hands and that the dog would be called off if he did so. Finally, he pulled out his hands and Merlin was released. The robber was handcuffed and dragged out to a police truck. We found the gun just inside the toilet.

The injuries this offender received were horrific but fully justified. If you play with guns then as far as I'm concerned the gloves are off. I want to go home to my family in one piece after every shift. Merlin had put four puncture wounds in the offender's penis. These ran from one side to the other. In addition, one of his testicles was hanging out of a tear in his scrotum. Merlin put a further six stitches in his thigh to add to the fourteen on his forehead. It's good to know that I have a dog who will protect me when the need arises. The armed robber was also relatively lucky, because without Merlin being there a likely outcome could have involved the police shooting him. To prove that this aggression is controlled, the next day I was rostered for a demonstration at Cabramatta High School. I put Merlin through his paces and gave a speech. I had Merlin chase out and retrieve his favourite toy. I took hold of it and swung him around lifting all four of his legs off the ground. He wouldn't let go and amazed the crowd with the power in his jaws and his determination never to give up or stop until I told him to. I got one of the kids to take the toy and hide it somewhere out of our sight at the back of their oval. I gave Merlin a command and he happily trotted off down the oval and returned to enthusiastic applause with the toy in his mouth. I could tell he was proud of himself as he had a very distinct spring in his step and his chest was puffed out making him look that little bit bigger. I was happy with him and equally proud. You have to understand that our dogs just want to make us happy—everything they do is done to make their 'dads' happy with them.

At the end, he happily sat there while school kids came up chatted with me and patted his big fat head. Not even a growl. Good boy.

The lure of drugs can be so great for some people they don't care or realise what's going on around them. There was one address where the junkies would literally line up at a window to buy their heroin. No matter how many times the police raided and searched the place arresting and charging the dealers, there was someone to take over the lucrative but evil trade. I decided one morning to go down and see who was hanging around. Merlin and I parked at Cabramatta Police Station and walked the kilometre to the block of units. Early in the morning watching people going off to work and taking their kids to school, we could have been in any suburb of Sydney except we were in Cabramatta and the drug trade was unfortunately rife.

Like all good drug dealers these guys had an early warning system for their business. They would have lookouts placed in strategic locations to warn of any impending police operation. To circumvent this, we would cut through the back of unit blocks and jump fences so as not to be seen. I would sneak through the side of a particular block and watch the drug window from behind a brick wall with Merlin sitting beside me. It didn't take long before the first customers started to line up at the window. They would shove money through a small hole and the heroin would be exchanged back out. The druggie would turn and get out of there as fast as possible before they were either searched by police or ripped off by another junkie. Usually they would jump a few fences and 'shoot up' in some poor bastard's backyard. My reasoning was that if there were no customers then there would be no business. If I could make coming here a real pain for the customers they would stop coming and the people who lived here would get a break from it. My actions were only going to be a tiny pinprick in the side of the drug trade here but it all has to start somewhere and sitting back doing nothing wasn't really an option for me. I waited until there were probably eight to ten customers lined up and charged out from behind the wall with Merlin straining on the lead in front of me. Most of them didn't see us until we were on the driveway. They shouted 'Cops' and scattered in all directions, jumping fences and tripping over each other in a mad panic. Merlin was barking and snapping his jaws at the running junkies. We followed a few over the fences and cleared the unit blocks two-deep on either side of the dealer's block. If one of them went to ground, Merlin found them and we chased them off again.

After ten minutes of this I was satisfied that they were all gone and returned to the window. I went up to it and bashed on the wooden frame which sat behind a steel grill. I yelled out, 'I'm going to be here all day, you're not going to make a cent today. If you've got a problem with that then come out and we'll have a chat.' Merlin chimed in too. barking and blocking his paws on the window frame. Unbelievably, while I was doing this, a druggie who was completely spaced out came and lined up behind me thinking I was another customer.

I turned to him and asked, 'What the hell are you doing here?'

His reply, 'Man, I'm just trying to get on' (meaning he was trying to buy some heroin).

I asked him if he knew who I was and to have a closer look if he was unsure. He squinted his eyes and all of a sudden a little light went on inside his head. 'Oh shit, man, I didn't realise it's the jacks man.' I just told him to start running and never come back here. Merlin gave him a verbal hurry up and he disappeared back onto the street. The only real consolation was that a resident of the unit block had been watching from the second storey and as I was leaving he gave me a wave and thumbs up. At least someone was happy.

These days Cabramatta is a very different place. It would be naive to think that the drug trade is gone but thanks to the efforts of many police sections and agencies, the drug problem is nowhere near as bad as it was.

A Very Nasty Surprise

It was about 6pm one evening in the middle of winter when we were called to an address in Lansvale. This is a suburb again right next to Cabramatta. The information I received was that there was a Break and Enter in progress and that the lady who lived in the house had come home to see the front door open. She had been attacked but had managed get to the neighbour's and ring the police. The call was that the offender was still inside. I arrived along with a number of Cabramatta police and went straight to the front door, which was open.

I gave Merlin a command and sent him inside. The lights were on and I could see him moving about the house searching from the front door. Bingo, I thought. I saw his tail wagging, head come up and ears pricked. He's found someone. But quite strangely, he wasn't barking at them. I could see him but not whatever it was that he was looking at. I told the others to wait and entered. He was near a kitchen area, which was darkened. I called him back and went in closer leaving him in a sitting position behind me. I saw a foot then a slipper. I moved in closer and saw the body of an elderly lady lying on the kitchen floor. I couldn't see properly and moved in much closer. I tried to wake her with a shake. Nothing. I asked if she could hear me. Nothing. I still couldn't see properly and reached over to check her neck for a pulse.

I felt my fingers slide right into the inside of her neck. Then I saw the huge pool of blood she was lying in. Her skin was clammy and getting cold. I looked closer and saw that my fingers had gone into the hole left by a wire garrot that had been used to strangle her. This had sliced open her throat from one side to the other. I shouted out for the ambulance officers to come in and help. They had been called to look after the daughter of this lady. Unfortunately she heard this and came running over. She had to be restrained and taken away. Someone had to tell the poor lady that her mother had been murdered. I'm glad it wasn't me because quite honestly I'm not sure that I could find the proper words. That is one of those crap jobs that police unfortunately have to do on a regular basis.

All that aside, I had to gather my thoughts and get moving. The offender had only left in the past ten minutes and we had a brief description to work on. I harnessed Merlin into his tracking gear and cast him across the front of the house. He gave me a very strong indication and started to track away from the house and down the street. Unfortunately we only tracked about 200m down the street and around a corner to an empty car space. The murderer was caught within a week. It was a person who had been threatening to kill both the old lady and her daughter. I can tell you that a dead body was the last and most unexpected thing that I thought Merlin would locate. I hope it doesn't happen again as these things tend to stick in your mind.

The next job in Cabramatta happened about 1am in the morning during summer. I was driving along Railway Parade outside the train station when a bloke with a black eye flagged me down. He told me that about ten guys who said they were from the 5T gang had just bashed him and stolen his wallet, mobile phone and bum bag. He told me he was from Melbourne and was trying to get to Parramatta but had accidentally got off at Cabramatta. When he asked these guys how to get to Parramatta they had bashed him and taken off with his property. He said that they had only just left on foot. I got him into my car and drove off in the direction they had gone.

About a minute later, we found them walking along the street laughing and carrying on. The guy from Melbourne started to panic. I told him not to worry. I called for other police to come to where we were and got Merlin out of the car. I walked over to the group and ordered them to sit on the ground. Merlin also put in his two cents worth and in no time they were all seated nicely where I could see them. I saw one of them throw a bum bag over a garden fence while we were waiting for the Cabramatta boys to turn up. I had forgotten to turn on my portable police radio while I was watching the ten from 5T. I had not heard the guy from Melbourne pick up the handset in the car and scream that the policeman with the dog needs help really quickly as the men he's stopped are armed with knives.

Of course the radio operator called a signal one (this means that every police officer that hears that kind of call drops whatever he or she is doing and gets to the scene as fast as possible and usually it means a brother police officer is in a life threatening situation) on my behalf thinking I was fighting ten offenders armed with knives, and I wasn't answering the radio. I was standing there with the thieves when I started to hear sirens, then more sirens, then a lot of sirens. There were cars coming from Fairfield, Cabramatta and even Blacktown police stations. I saw the first Cabramatta truck come around the corner sideways with its lights flashing and sirens blaring. Then a few more in the same fashion. I suppose I stood there with a dumb look on my face as the police piled out and ran up to us.

I asked them what the hell was going on? They told me what had been said over the radio and there were cars coming from everywhere.

I put their minds at ease and turned on my radio explaining to the operator that it was the victim of the assault who had called on the radio without my knowledge and that I was going to have a little word with him. I stormed over to the car and gave it to him with both barrels explaining that those criminals that had robbed him were no problem for me and my dog and that if they had tried it on with us then it would have been an unpleasant experience for them. Also that I was able to make decisions as to whether I'm in trouble or not. By his actions he had made police drive on urgent duty without a proper reason and that they had better things to do than come running over here. The upshot was that the offenders were arrested and charged with a number of offences and he got all his stolen possessions back.

The last incident from Cabramatta wasn't really a dog catch but rather the result of bad acting and stupidity by a couple of thieves. It was during the day and I was walking around the car park of the Kookaburra Hotel in Canley Vale. At the time there was a fair degree of criminal activity going on in this car park including drug dealing, car theft and break-ins.

I saw a brand new Magna pull up and a man and woman climbed out. I was one car from them when the female walked past me. Usually people look at Merlin whether they're hoodlums or law-abiding people. This idiot put her nose in the air and walked past trying to ignore the fact that we were there. The man was even worse. He looked like someone had inserted a large pointy pole up his backside and walked past as stiff as a board. 'Come here, mate, I want to talk to you,' I said.

Something wasn't right about these two and the type of car they had arrived in. I saw that he had a fit box, which is a black plastic container for syringes, in his hand. He also had the keys to the Magna, which he dropped thinking that I hadn't seen him do it. By now he was shaking like a leaf. I asked him whether he owned the car and his reply was, 'What car?' I made him sit down while Merlin watched him.

I retrieved the keys and turned to the crook, 'The Magna, you know because you just dropped the keys.' I did a transport check which revealed that this car had been stolen from a house after a Break and Enter a week ago, and also it had been used by a male and female in numerous other Break and Enters and bag snatches since then. I used the keys that opened the car revealing a treasure trove of stolen property.

I placed him under arrest and put a description of the female over the police radio. She was picked up about five minutes later trying to get on a train at Canley Vale Rail Station. I had to hand the arrest over to the Cabramatta Detectives, as there were a lot of enquiries to be made. Most of the property was returned to the rightful owners.

It's Not Only Cats Who Have Nine Lives

I t was mid-winter, night-time, and we were called to an intruder alarm at a multi-storey office block on the Pacific Highway at Gordon in Sydney's north. The attending police did all the right things and set up a good perimeter. All I had to do was go in and let my hairy mate search the place. Initially all went well and Merlin was trotting in and out of the offices on all the floors searching for offenders. Nothing inside so I decided to start searching the multi-level car park which was incorporated in the building.

I started on the fourth and top level of the car park. There was a strong breeze blowing and all of a sudden Merlin started to indicate human scent from the direction of a car, which was parked along the outside wall of the car park. I thought, beauty there's someone inside or underneath that car. All of a sudden, Merlin jumped up and went over the side rail of the car park. As he was doing so I screamed out, 'NO!', but over he went. I saw his life and my career in the Dog Squad flash in front of my eyes. Merlin had actually picked up the scent of a police officer who had been standing beside the building four storeys down. The breeze had carried it up.

I ran over and looked down expecting to see the worst. Instead I saw

Merlin walking around on a mound of grass clippings and cut branches beside an ashen-faced constable. I put him into a down position and ran down. Not a single bloody scratch or limp, he was fine. I couldn't believe it. He'd almost landed on the officer who said all she saw was a black mass falling towards her and heard me screaming out. I took him straight to the car and finished the job. I believe that there are some people in the world who are quite simply blessed and Merlin is one of them.

If I Knew I Wouldn't Have Bothered

There were two building searches that I wouldn't have let Merlin do on his own if I had known what was inside. The first was a certain large supermarket in a certain Sydney suburb. It was about four in the morning and there had been a Break and Enter with the front glass doors smashed for entry. I arrived and sent Merlin in for a search. He did something unusual; he ran straight down the back of the store and disappeared into the dark. I initially thought that he had located someone in the store. After about five minutes I hadn't heard anything and he hadn't returned. Usually if he doesn't return it means he's found something and if he's not talking, he may be fighting with someone.

I walked in and started to look. Nothing. I went through the rear plastic doors into a butchery. That's when I started to become suspicious that maybe Police Dog Merlin was doing something that maybe he shouldn't be doing. I stopped and listened. There it was, I heard a dog panting and eating. You little bastard. I switched on my torch and started to look. I could hear him but couldn't see him. Then I saw an ear and half a head. Where were these parts of a very bad dogs anatomy, I hear you asking? Inside a wheelie bin full of all kinds of meat and bone off-cuts. To his credit, he came straight out and to my side very gingerly when I asked. He knew he was a bad boy and that I had a huge case of the shits with him. So it was straight into the car and away. 'Nothing in there,' I said, as I drove away very quickly.

The next pointless search was at a huge warehouse in Blacktown. Again it was early in the morning and we had been called to search the building. It was very dark and all I knew was that someone may be inside. Again I sent him in for a search and waited at the point of entry for the thieves, which happened to be a panel they had pulled off from the outside of the wall. He ran inside and soon disappeared into the darkness. I couldn't hear him panting or running but wasn't worried, as this place was the size of about ten football fields. I waited for about ten minutes and still nothing. Soon after, the manager of the building turned up and offered to turn on all the lights. I agreed and was going to wait for light before I went in. I couldn't work out why this manager looked at me funnily when I said that my dog was searching. Then the lights came on and I realised why he was now laughing. There were ten football fields worth of dog food stacked fifty meters high inside this warehouse. I thought to myself that little bugger, he's in doggy heaven and unsupervised. I called for him and about two minutes later he appeared. I just put him in the car and again beat a hasty retreat. I didn't want to know what he'd been up to this time.

Tree Huggers

As dog handlers, we spend a lot of time patrolling schools after hours. Unfortunately many criminals see schools as soft targets full of computers that are easy to take and sell off. They do not realise that these crimes affect many people including tax payers and most importantly the children who have to do without vital learning equipment at school.

We like to get in there and sneak around, hopefully catching them in the act. One night in summer I was walking around a school in Parramatta not far from Police Headquarters. I let Merlin off his lead and watched as he disappeared into the darkness. He would let me know if anything was going on. After about five minutes I had heard nothing and called him back. Nothing. I called again and started to walk towards the centre of the school. I finally saw him 100m away wagging his tail and looking up into a tree. I thought, little bugger he's chased a cat or a possum up the tree. I called him but he kept circling and started to bark, not very convincingly. I walked over and shone the torch up the tree to find to my surprise a man and woman about twenty years old hugging each other on one of the branches. Both were well dressed in business suits. I said, 'It's the police, come down.' I put Merlin on lead and watched as they sheepishly climbed down looking at us ashen faced. I asked them what they had been doing in the school. I didn't think they had been doing anything wrong but I was curious and trying not to laugh. I got an answer that did end up making me chuckle. 'We were having a kiss on the bench here under the tree when your dog came up and jumped in between us and licked my girlfriend's face. I went to push him away and he started to growl. I shit myself and jumped up the tree along with her until you arrived.'

I laughed and reminded them that schools are out of bounds to everyone no matter what the reason and sent them on their way.

Car Jacking

It was a lovely spring afternoon in Sydney and I had just started an afternoon shift. In fact I was still at a park near my house giving Merlin a chance to relieve himself before we headed out on the road. There had been a car jacking in Albert Ave Chatswood in Sydney's north. The car jacker had walked up to the window of a car and asked the driver for directions. When he leaned over to retrieve his map the driver had a knife put to his throat. He was flung out and the offender drove away. Fortunately this occurred near Chatswood Police Station and a description of the car in question was put over the police radio network literally in minutes.

About five minutes later a Highway Patrol vehicle spotted the car driving south on the Sydney Harbour Bridge. They were in an unmarked V8 Falcon and followed him across. Can you believe the crook even stopped to pay the toll! A few minutes later he twigged and a pursuit was started through the city. I was a long way north of this and didn't think that I'd be of any use. However police radio called for a dog and I was the only one who was able to respond at that time. I radioed and said that I would get to the pursuit as fast as possible. I could hear the call from the Highway car. They were driving at mayhem speed through the centre of the city. I was travelling at a good warp speed and found myself at North Ryde when the pursuit finally ended in Ashfield about 10km from the city. The thief had hit a gutter and blown a front tyre. He leaped out and ran over fences. He was last seen by the Highway Patrol police going into a council depot full of trucks and maintenance buildings. Luckily there were about ten police cars in this pursuit when it had finished and a very good perimeter was set. The highway guys also did the right thing, as they knew I was coming and stopped chasing him when he went into the depot. Unfortunately for the fugitive, one of the buildings that ran along the side of the depot was a police station.

When I heard what had happened I put my foot to the floor and made the trip from the Hornsby area to Ashfield in peak-hour traffic in 12 minutes. Every second counts in dog handling. I arrived and was shown the fence where the crook had last been seen. As he was possibly armed I started a search with Merlin on his normal lead. I didn't want him being stabbed. We walked the perimeter and found nothing. There was a small breeze blowing through the depot, which was about 100x200m. There were office buildings on one side and an undercover parking area with about fifteen garbage and dump trucks parked in it.

All of a sudden Merlin put his nose in the air and hackled up. He started to growl and pulled me towards the undercover parking area. I yelled out, 'Police, come out or I'll send the dog!' I gave a command and off he raced. He bolted straight down to the trucks with me and the highway officer right behind him. We stopped and watched him do his magic. He ran in large circles to begin with, narrowing it down until he was circling a dump truck that was full of tree branches. Merlin was trying to get in but the side of the truck was way too high for him. He was barking and going crazy. I knew we had him. I put Merlin into a sit and climbed onto the tailgate. Looking in I couldn't see a thing so I made it easy for myself. 'Okay, come out or I'll put the dog in here and he'll make you come out.' One second later, a pair of hands appeared from under the branches and the thief emerged.

It still amazes me that a dog can pick the scent from a person who is 100m away hiding under a pile of branches in the back of a dump truck with its tailgate up. I was very happy with that result and suitably let all the other handlers I saw know how good Merlin was. (Just ask any handler and he'll tell you that it's actually him and his dog that are the best in the squad.)

Damn Fence

One of the few downsides of being a dog handler is that you are constantly climbing walls, fences and gates, crawling under and over buildings and running through the bush at night bashing into things. This tends to dish out a few injuries. There isn't a dog handler in the squad who hasn't had some kind of injury at one time or another. I was doing what I thought was a pretty routine job at a house in Burwood. The owner had disturbed an intruder when he came home. They had run out the back door and over his fence into a school. I arrived and got a track going with Merlin in the backyard.

We reached the fence and I stopped and looked over. It was about four feet on our side, but ten feet to the ground on the other side. Merlin was fired up and leaped over without any problems. I put him in a sit position on the other side and started to climb the fence. I sat on the top and started to lower myself over. This is when the world turned to shit for me. My belt became looped over one of the fence palings. I was momentarily stuck there, which was no problem until I heard the sound of wood splintering. I guess it wasn't built to take over 100kg of equipment and me. The paling broke and I dropped with it. I fell on an angle to my left. All my weight came down on my left leg. I heard a horrible squelch then a snap from my left knee.

I tried to get up but it was all over and I was in a lot of pain. I have to admit that I swore at the top of my voice when I realised what I had done. Merlin came over to my cussing body and licked my face, barked as if to say 'come on dad, the crook's gone this way'. Well I wasn't going anywhere. I had to call it on the police radio and get an ambulance. This was fine except for one thing, Merlin. He sat by me and wouldn't let anybody come near. He snapped at the other police and ambulance officers. We had to call another handler to come and take him away. As we were waiting, of course it started to rain. I couldn't get mad at Merlin because he was just looking out for me.

Anyway I had to have a knee reconstruction and was away from work for about six months. This included Merlin who was looked after by other handlers while I recuperated. They did a really good job but I became very depressed. The first week or so is alright but after that sitting around becomes a bore. I just wanted my dog back and to go out on the road. It was a very painful and frustrating process. It has taken about two years for me to become totally pain free but at least I could get around. The day Merlin came back it was as if he had never left. He came in, jumped all over me then gave me a dog slobber facial. Just like he owned the joint he went over, sat on his mat and went to sleep.

A Shot in the Dark

I was patrolling around my old stamping grounds in Redfern's patrol on a mid-winter night shift. There had been a couple of pursuits with stolen high-performance cars and I was sniffing around hoping to get Merlin into a position to catch the drivers. I was trawling along backstreets of Waterloo in the car at very low speed with the lights off in an effort to try and surprise anyone who was up to no good. I was just about to give up and try something else when a call came over for a man dressed in a white coat and white hat firing a rifle into the air. This was happening only about a kilometre from where we were. This type of job has a double effect on me. First, I'm excited at the prospect of being close and having a good chance of finding him. Second, I get a sinking feeling in my stomach knowing that this guy might shoot at us and end it all if we are able to confront or corner him.

Either way, I'm paid to do a job and these are the situations where you have to get past your doubts and fears and earn your money. When you join the cops you have to accept that one day you might get shot at.

I switched on the headlights and headed over to where he had last been seen. I was the first police car off in the street but couldn't see anything obvious. A lady called down from her balcony telling me that the 'Guy with the gun went that way' and pointed to a corner

200m away. Right at that moment, I heard what sounded like a distant gunshot. I put the information over the police radio and drove to the corner. The entire area is full of high-rise apartments and terrace houses which means there are lots of people in a relatively small area. The laws of gravity state that what goes up must come down and a bullet has a good chance of coming down on someone's head in this area. I put on my full ballistic vest and harnessed Merlin into his tracking gear.

Again another shot rang out but it was impossible to try and get a location or distance due to the high rises. I gave Merlin his command, he put his nose to the ground and started to track this maniac's scent. I felt a bit better when a Tactical Operations Unit van pulled up alongside. These are just the guys you want backing you up when there are offenders with long arms on the loose. They said they were going to shadow us and confront the gunman if we located him. Sounded good to me. Another shot rang out as we tracked along but it still seemed to be a fair way off. The track went in and out of unit blocks and through back streets for about five minutes.

There was a call soon after from a local Redfern crew saying they had spotted a male matching the description on Phillip Street, Waterloo. I was still about 400m from there and continued on behind Merlin who was steadily tracking along oblivious to the danger which may not have been too far ahead.

A few minutes more and the crew from Redfern had pulled up, rushed him and taken him into custody. They let us know over the radio that he was the shooter but the gun was nowhere to be found. They could smell the cordite from the fired rounds on his hands and clothing, and he even had a few .45 calibre rounds in his pocket but he refused to admit that he had fired any gun. I lost a bit of the tension that I had been carrying throughout the track. I could concentrate more on Merlin and what he was doing and not so much on looking ahead making sure the gunman wasn't lining us up. Merlin tracked strongly down the side of a two-storey block of units about 100m from where the male was stopped.

Suddenly he stopped and stuck his nose behind a wheelie bin. I could tell by his body language that he was telling me something was behind there. I told him he was a good boy and put him in a sit position, pulled the bin back and bingo, there was a lever action .45 calibre rifle propped up against the wall. I turned back again and let Merlin know that he was making me very happy indeed. I put the location of the rifle over the police radio then continued the track as we still needed to know whether the gun belonged to the man who had been stopped. Merlin picked the scent up straight away and hoovered his way straight up to where the male protesting his innocence was standing. We went around him and tried to pick a scent anywhere past where he was standing. Nothing. Merlin didn't indicate anything in any direction past where he was standing. I walked straight up to where the arresting police and gunman were standing and I said, 'He's the one, mate I found your gun behind the wheelie bin.' He kept on denying it as he was put in the back of the truck and taken away to be charged. Even if he hadn't been stopped on the night we would have found the gun and lifted his prints off it. Good police work all around from everyone meant that we didn't have to wait.

A Simple Domestic

Domestic violence is an ugly part of society which police have to deal with on a regular basis. It is not linked to any particular socio-economic group. Rich or poor, smart or stupid, it's everywhere. These situations are probably the most dangerous that an officer can face. Emotions are running high and the police have to come into a couple's house, take over and sort it out, usually to find a few weeks down the track when it comes time to go to court, that the couple have kissed and made up and don't want to go on with it. This is very frustrating as you know full well it's going to happen again.

I was on afternoon shift in the Parramatta area. There wasn't much going on and a call came over about a violent domestic disturbance just around the corner from where we were. I arrived with a local police crew and went into the unit. We found a motorcycle in the front hallway of the unit and two very upset ladies in the lounge room with some very nasty bruises and cuts to their faces. The ex-boyfriend of one of the ladies had started to hit her when she refused to keep the stolen motorcycle in her unit. The young lady's mother stepped in and was also punched and slapped. He then dragged them both out the front by their hair and started to bash their heads together until they both fell down (lovely bloke). He had heard the sirens coming and had taken off with a friend who was waiting in a car. The first lady told us that the ex had been drinking rum and beer all day as well as using amphetamines. She also warned us that he hated police and in his current state would put on a fight if confronted. She then informed us she knew where he was. I told the officers from Granville I'd go along with them just in case he ran.

So we took the first lady and headed over to an address in Parramatta. I parked further down the street from the other police and started to walk up to where they were standing. I could see that they were talking to a male who was very solid and about six feet tall. As I drew closer I could see that he was arguing with them and was becoming agitated. I was still about ten feet away when he threw a punch at the male officer. He moved and jumped on the assailant's back. Unfortunately, the officer was only about eighty kilos and much smaller than the crook. His partner was female and about twenty kilos lighter than him. However both have very big hearts and started to struggle with this violent maniac who was up to his eyeballs in alcohol and amphetamines. Then, just to make things very interesting, I saw him reach into his pocket and try to pull out a 30cm carving knife, which he had taken from his ex's kitchen. The first officer was still riding him around like a rodeo rider while the second officer had just been kicked quite literally into the bushes. I screamed for the officer to let go and get off him. He still had not seen the knife and was giving me a very questioning look. I was convinced that he was about to stab my colleague. Merlin was going beserk and champing at the bit to take him on. I yelled out 'KNIFE!'

The first officer jumped off and moved away. I moved in closer with Merlin who immediately bit the drug-fuelled lunatic on his forearm. Thankfully, it was the arm with which he was holding the knife and even more thankfully he dropped it. I was ordering him to the ground but he wasn't listening or feeling any pain whatsoever. He was given a dose of capsicum spray by both of the other police, he was being bitten by a police dog and struck to his legs with a baton by me. He just stood there and laughed. The amphetamines were doing their job. He thought he was invincible and could not feel any of the pain being inflicted on him. He was continually punching Merlin and the other two police were screaming that he was going to kill us.

Eventually Merlin took one step back after biting his arms and legs. It looked like he made a conscious decision that this wasn't working and he'd have to change tactics. He then launched himself back at this lunatic and took him by the groin. This actually made him scream and lower his guard. I managed to get in a punch to his jaw while the other two grabbed an arm each. He went down and the other two managed to handcuff him to the rear. I immediately released Merlin's grip and moved about 2m away. Once the cuffs are on an offender on the ground there isn't any need or justification to keep the dog on him. By this stage I was quite buggered—fighting is an energy sapping business. The offender had calmed down and was having a conversation with the two other police telling them that he was going to be good now and behave.

They stood him up and immediately he kicked the female constable to her stomach, which literally sent her flying through the air about a metre into a brick wall (unfortunately she was becoming a bit of a frequent flyer). He turned and kicked the male officer who disappeared through a hedge. Then he turned to me and screamed that he was going to kill the dog and me. I was still standing about 2m away and told him in no uncertain terms that if he did that I was going to hurt him. He took no notice and charged straight into us kicking Merlin about three times hard to his head and chest. This not only angered Merlin but made me bloody angry. He was handcuffed but had shown that he was very proficient with his legs and still posed a real threat to my safety. I let Merlin go and grabbed his arm. Merlin bit into his right leg which was by now bleeding very heavily from puncture and tear wounds inflicted by Merlin previously. Unbelievably, he kept trying to knee me and bite my face and I had no choice but to let him have it with my baton. The only way to stop this maniac was going to be by taking him down mechanically.

In the meantime, Merlin had a good hold of his right ankle and I could see that he was tearing off chunks of meat. The two other very gutsy officers had recovered and joined in. Again he was put on the ground. By this stage more police had arrived and helped us put him in the rear of a police caged truck. He was refused service at Westmead Hospital because he was too violent. The ambulance officers managed to patch him up in the cells at Parramatta. We had inflicted some very heavy duty damage to him, especially Merlin who I think has probably given him a permanent limp by chewing up his Achilles tendon. Apparently when he woke up the next morning he was very sore and asked the police on duty what had happened and why was he there and so sore all over. At least he had the decency to plead guilty to all the offences relating to assaulting police and cruelty to animals.

Even though it's my job to bring criminals to justice I have respect for those that face up to what they have done and cop it on the chin when they take us on and lose.

Escapee

It was 4am and I was heading home from Fairfield in Sydney's west. I decided to go through Parramatta and up Pennant Hills Road towards home. I changed to the police channel, which covered this area and immediately heard a call from a very frantic sounding custody manager from a certain police station. 'He got out of the cells and escaped from the station.' This offender had just been arrested for fifteen armed robberies and was in the cells waiting to be charged by detectives after a gruelling marathon interview. This guy was young but looking at many, many years behind bars. The custody manager had just walked him back to his cell and thought he had locked the door properly. He had been distracted and called to the front counter of the station. The next thing he knew he saw the same criminal come out of a fire escape door, give him the one fingered salute and run off down the street like his pants were on fire.

I was able to press the pedal on the police car pretty hard and arrived about two minutes later. This was a serious situation and we had to get this dangerous armed robber back into custody before he could hurt anybody again. I cast a frantic Merlin who had picked up the vibe of the situation in the area where the escapee was last seen. He scoured the ground with his nose and eventually got the scent we were after. We tracked over about six fences, and each time we went over one Merlin seemed to pick up his pace as the distance between our quarry and us dissipated. Soon we came to a Colorbond fence which was about 5m high. Merlin was starting to growl and I knew this guy was very close. How am I going to get him over this bloody fence, I thought but I didn't have to worry because Merlin made the decision for me. He had gone to the edge where a small portion of the fence had been pushed in. He put his head in and pushed it further knocking a big hole which opened up enough for him to barge through then drag me eyes shut and swearing through the same slim gap. It made a hell of a racket as the entire aluminium sheet came crashing down. I'm still amazed that I wasn't sliced open by the sharp edges.

Merlin didn't stop to ask how I was as he dragged me around a corner and began barking at a space under a wheelie bin. I shouted, 'Police come out now or the dog's coming in.' I repeated myself when I got no reply. I knew he was in there and I was determined that Merlin and I were going to take all the happiness out of his day. He decided to come out. First I saw a pair of hands that were noticeably shaking come up out from behind the wheelie bin. Then a pair of noodle arms attached to a skinny torso. I was expecting a big, hard, tattoo-covered criminal to appear. Instead, I got a skinny little druggie who was crying and wet his pants right there in front of me. I handcuffed him and marched him back out to the other police who had been enforcing a perimeter around the entire block ensuring there was little chance for his escape.

The custody manager at this police station was a very relieved man. He had smoked about thirty cigarettes in the space of the ten minutes that the job had taken. He very enthusiastically told me that he would be eternally grateful to the Dog Squad. I was glad that we were in the right place at the right time and able to help out.

The Mole

This story starts with Operation West Safe, which is a highway patrol operation that involves the saturation of an area by Highway Patrol officers for all kinds of enforcement including random breath testing and speed checks. On this particular night it was being run in the Fairfield area. I like to hang around these operations, as there are usually pursuits and offenders running on foot. This night was no different.

The highway officers had a random breath test stop set up on the Cumberland Highway just opposite the Fairfield West Public School. A truck had been stopped and the driver breath tested. The officer became suspicious of the driver as he appeared very nervous. When asked for his driver's licence the driver pretended to look for it, put the truck into gear and took off with the officer still standing on the outside step of the truck's cabin. As the truck gained speed the officer was flung off suffering a few cuts and bruises as the driver turned left off the highway. He stopped the truck about 20m up the road and ran off along a steep driveway into houses and disappeared into the dark.

I was called and turned up about five minutes later passing the ambulance officers who were treating the injured officer. Luckily there were a lot of police in the immediate vicinity so a quick perimeter had been put up on all the streets surrounding the block where he had last been seen. I was pretty confident and started to search. I couldn't track as the initial police at the scene had run into the area where he had last run. We started to search from house to house and garden to garden. Merlin wasn't showing much interest in any of these yards. I was about to go back and start searching in a different direction when we reached the last house on the block. I spoke to the officers at the front who told me they had already been in there and searched with a negative result. I decided to send Merlin in anyway just to make sure, as dog handlers we like to be sure in our own minds that everything has been covered.

There was no moon and all the lights in this yard were off. It was pitch black. I watched Merlin run over to a garden bed and start growling. I turned on the torch but I couldn't see a thing. Then he started to dig, wagging his tail in excitement. Soon after he had something in his mouth and was dragging it out from the hole he had dug. To my amazement it was an arm, with the driver attached to it. This guy had buried himself in the loose dirt and was breathing through a hole he had left in it. The highway officers came in and were just as amazed as they told me that they had both stood on the garden bed to see into the next yard. He was fully removed from the garden, smelling and looking dirty and dishevelled as he was handcuffed and dragged away. No wonder he tried so hard. He was wanted in Queensland and New South Wales for some serious drug and property offences. We got him here first and after he has been finished with in New South Wales he'll be sent to Queensland for some banana bending justice. Bad luck for a bad boy.

Not While You're on the Job

We had been called to Neutral Bay on the lower North Shore of Sydney after two offenders had been disturbed breaking into a newly built house at four in the morning. Both had run off and were hiding somewhere around a block of units and parkland nearby. I arrived and started to walk down an alleyway with Merlin when a head appeared from behind a brick retaining wall. He had a good look and turned to run. I shouted out, 'Police, don't bother running or I'll release the dog.' Merlin was barking and champing at the bit to go. This thief had been around a while and had probably dealt with police dogs before. He stopped, giving himself up without a fight.

We started to search the area but we couldn't find the second offender. There was one fence that Merlin kept stopping at and appeared to be interested in. As this was the only indication he was giving I decided to get in and have a look. Because this is a very affluent part of Sydney, most of the houses have very high walls and locked fortress-like gates. I managed to get us up onto a sandstone ledge, which was six feet off the ground, then jumped/threw Merlin over the remaining eight foot brick fence, which ran around the house. I couldn't see over the other side and hoped that it wasn't too far for him to jump. When he disappeared I heard the sound of crashing paint tins and other debris that he must have gone through. I climbed to the top and saw him run off from the side of the house towards the backyard which was in total darkness.

I very carefully lowered myself the eight to ten feet down the other side and crept along the side wall towards the rear yard. I couldn't see or hear anything. I was just beginning to wonder what had happened to Merlin when I saw a shadow on the rear deck of the house. I stopped and heard some very heavy dog panting along with another dog making a kind of low growling noise. I put the torch in the direction of the shadow and didn't know whether to laugh or cry. There was Merlin mounted on top of a female German shepherd having his way with her. I tried to be as quiet as possible and called him to me. He just stared at me and kept on going. I was trying to be as quiet as possible and moved in closer. Even though he's my dog it's very dangerous to try and take him off forcibly during sex. I know I'd take exception and he's no different. Just as I was contemplating what to do, the people inside the house came to the back door and turned on the outside lights. Unfortunately they saw what was going on and came straight out. The man of the house just looked at the two dogs, then at me and asked what the hell was going on.

I have to admit I stumbled with my words and eventually got out that we were looking for a person who had committed a Break and Enter. He then asked why my dog was 'raping' his dog. He told me that his dog was on heat but it was no excuse for this happening. I might remind you all at this point that Merlin was still working away with his little girlfriend while this conversation was taking place. I started to apologise. Then he finished what he was doing and walked off into the yard leaving the bitch there on the deck. I quickly put him on lead and asked to be let out. I told the man that Merlin's bloodlines were impeccable and that any pups would be real champions. He grunted and let us out. I wasn't sure whether I should be cranky at Merlin or give him a high five so I put him in the car and reported that nothing had been found. Wasn't it W.C. Fields who advised never to work with children or animals?

New Year's Eve

I have been very lucky in the Dog Squad because I've only had to work on one New Year's Eve. This has been quite enjoyable as every other one I've spent in the City area watching everyone else have fun. On the year that I had to work I was sent up to the Central Coast town of Terrigal. Every year they block off the main street to traffic and have a huge party on the beach promenade and street. Of course as the night wears on people become more and more drunk and out of control. Then it's the poor bloody coppers who have to step in and restore order. On nights like this it usually means the police are outnumbered by about a hundred to one. A police dog helps to even up the odds a bit.

The worst thing about being in or near a large, intoxicated crowd is that everyone wants to pat the dog or come up and think they can intimidate the dog and handler. I'm constantly checking behind us and watching for these idiots to come in. One such fool came in from our left side, which is the side that Merlin is always on. He walked right into Merlin and was promptly bitten on his backside. I grabbed him and threw him at the two police who were standing there with us. I said, 'What the hell did you do that for?' He replied, 'I thought it was a drug dog, I don't have any drugs so I thought I'd be okay.' I told him what I thought of him and his obviously empty head and sent him on his way. After midnight when most of the families had left, the whole thing started to get ugly with very large groups of young males and some females walking around looking to start fights. One such group clashed with another.

This melee involved about fifty people who were then joined by all the onlookers who were egging them on. Stuck right in the middle of all this were about six police officers. They tried to break up the fight and were turned on by both the warring parties who had now become allied in the fight against the police. At the time I was around the corner and heard a very dramatic call for urgent assistance on the police radio. I ran around and saw the police who were trying to arrest two of the main offenders. They were surrounded by the rest of the mob who were starting to throw empty glass beer bottles at them. Only one thing for it, charge! I started yelling at the crowd to move or the dog was going to move them. It's amazing how fast you can clear an area with a 40kg German shepherd. I managed to move the crowd back about 2m. Unfortunately they started to throw bottles at me. I felt a couple whistle past my head. If any of them had connected with mine or any other police officer's head these morons would be up on serious charges—being drunk and an imbecile is no defence in court. Luckily most of them missed and only a few injuries were inflicted on the police.

All of a sudden one drunk came right out in front of the crowd and threw a bottle straight at me. It just missed, and he started to laugh with his mates who were egging him on. He then reached into his shorts pocket and dragged out another one. He was about to throw it so I charged forward and let Merlin give it to him. Merlin gave him a bite right on the inside of his thigh then took hold of his shorts. I was dragging him back towards the police line while his mates had his arms and were dragging him back towards them. The gods were truly

A day to remember—the first day I was teamed up with Merlin.

Police dogs are trained to hang on to an offender until they are given a command to let go.

The NSW Police Dog Squad official photo of Merlin and me.

Police dogs go through rigorous training exercises to keep them fit and strong. Pleasing their handlers is all the motivation they need.

Merlin could clamber over just about any obstacle
in his determination to catch a crook.

Police dogs can't tell the difference between a uniformed officer and a criminal. When they are commanded to apprehend an 'offender', they do so without hesitation.

Merlin's favourite place to hang out at home.
The boards are worn from him lying in this spot.

Merlin and I formed a close bond—an essential ingredient
for police dogs and their handlers to be a successful team.

*Merlin was one of the family in no time
and was as much a family pet as he was a working dog.*

Just like a police officer's uniform, police dogs are expected to be kept neat and clean. This was not one of Merlin's favourite parts of the job.

with us that night because the next thing I know Merlin managed to pull off his pants revealing that he was not wearing any underwear. He was last seen running up the main street half naked and bleeding from his leg. I'd like to have charged him but he was never seen again. This incident also had the effect of dispersing the crowd along with the help of a large number of police who had by now turned up. The main thing was that as police we had worked as a team and arrested who needed to be arrested, and all been able to go home in one piece.

There was another New Year's Eve incident this time in Sydney. I had been driving around all night and occasionally getting out for a walk. I stopped that after the second walk. I was losing patience after saying Happy New Year for the five thousandth time to everyone who was having a great night and a few sherberts while I was working with a self-imposed dark cloud over my grump of a head.

It was now about 2am and I was driving very slowly down under the northern end of the Sydney Harbour Bridge. The crowd had thinned out a bit, but there were still plenty of revellers clogging the roads and park. Merlin was staring out the side window barking at everyone who came too close to the car for his liking (another reason for my headache and crappy mood). All of a sudden a lady came shooting out of the crowd and banged madly on the windscreen of the car. I stopped and wound down my window wondering whether she was just a drunk looking for a lift or if there was something I could help her with. She just blurted out, 'Come quick, there are two police officers surrounded under the bridge, hurry.'

This woke me up and out of my mood in a millisecond. I jumped out and collected Merlin from the back of the car. He had a big stretch then trotted along at my side. The lady pointed to an area under the pylons where I could now see two female police officers with their backs to the pylon wall. They were surrounded by about ten to fifteen males who, even from this distance, were obviously threatening them. As we came in closer, I could see that all the males in the group were from a certain background that only likes to confront other people when the numbers are well and truly stacked in their own favour. I was starting to pick up what was being said by the group. They were threatening to kill and sexually assault the two female police officers who were standing with their backs to the wall, police batons in hand. The group of males were not letting them move but also didn't have the intestinal fortitude to go too close. They were trying to use their police radio to call for back up but for whatever reason none of their transmissions were working. None of the cowardly group had seen us walk up behind them—they were too intent on trying to intimidate the police in front of them. (Mind you, none of them still had the guts to get into baton range.) I let them go on for a minute after my two colleagues had seen me there with my black-and-tan taser. It had been hard work but I managed to keep Merlin quiet, then I decided it was time to act and I knew exactly what was going to happen. I walked up about a metre and a half from the back of the first coward and I yelled, 'POLICE! IF YOU TAKE ONE OF US ON YOU TAKE ALL OF US ON!'

The closest coward jumped into the air with a little scream when he got the full brunt of my challenge and Merlin's barking frenzy in unison. I asked the two police if they wanted any of them to be arrested. They said 'no let's just get rid of them.' The rest of them, as I expected, went to water and started to run for their lives. It was a lesson to them that if you take on one cop then you take on all the cops and every asset we have. Merlin ensured that they were made to look like the cowards that they were. He dragged me after them snapping and growling at their quickly retreating backsides. Fifteen of them verses the two police officers and us and I think the odds were still in our favour. We chased them through the crowd and up towards Milsons Point railway station, not allowing any of them to stop or slow down. In the end we chased them off onto the Pacific Highway and out of sight. Merlin wanted to keep on going but I'd had enough and we walked back to where it had all started. It doesn't happen often but we got some applause and cheers from the crowd as we weaved our way back. Merlin was in his 'I'm a tough guy' trot and had his chest puffed out accordingly. I found the two constables who had been surrounded outside the rail station helping the ambos with an unconscious reveller. It turns out that they had been with a larger group of police, some of whom had been involved in another arrest and left the area to take care of that. These two had volunteered to stay in the area until the others had returned. It doesn't matter whether you're a big cop or a small cop, we all work as a team complementing each other's skills and strengths. We returned to the car satisfied that we had welcomed in the New Year doing what we love to do.

Another Mole

I don't know what it is about the Highway Patrol and how desperate they make people they are chasing become but this story shows it again. I was up on the Central Coast about thirty minutes drive from Sydney. We were in the suburb of Woy Woy assisting with a joint traffic and Break and Enter operation.

About midnight we heard a call over the police radio from a Highway Patrol vehicle, 'Brisbane Waters 202 urgent we're in pursuit of a vehicle that's just run the Random Breath Testing station.' They continued to call the locations and speeds until the car, a brand new Honda Prelude, crashed with the driver running off into an alley behind a couple of blocks of houses. I wasn't far behind and Merlin who sensed something was on was barking and whining inside his cage. I arrived and saw the passenger side of the Prelude wrapped around a telegraph pole, airbags deployed and the engine smoking. A total write-off. I spoke to the Highway officers who said they pulled up behind him slowly as they didn't think he was going to walk away from the crash and, looking at the remains of the car, I could see why. All they could tell me was he was wearing a red shirt and had a beard. I got Merlin and harnessed him up right next to the driver's door. He was champing at the bit to get going and by the way he was spinning around and growling I could tell this guy was not far ahead.

I gave him his command and he put his nose to the ground sucking up the scent and grass as we went. He was pulling me along very powerfully, taking the corners like a Formula One car. We tracked off the street of the crash and into a side alley which led in behind a row of houses then out into an open grass area. Merlin slowed up and started to move in circles, meaning that the track had changed direction or that the driver was very close. All I could see was the row of houses with a log wood retaining wall opposite which led up on to another open grass area. Merlin was growling and started to pull me towards the retaining wall, wagging his tail and pumping out his chest. This guy was definitely very close and probably lying there wishing he was somewhere else. We jumped up on to the retaining wall. I expected to see the driver lying flat on the grass but there was nothing and Merlin wasn't going any further. Instead he dragged me over to a part of the wall and barked down into a small opening. He even started to dig with his paws to get to whoever was hiding there. I pulled him back and lit the hole. There he was, well his shoes at least. They were, however, attached to his feet and therefore the rest of his body. I called on him to come out but he told me he was stuck between the logs and the earth wall. I put Merlin in a sit position then started to pull the driver out. I could smell the alcohol seeping from every pore in his body. After a couple minutes of hard pulling by me and whining by him, I had the driver out and under arrest. He was very drunk and covered from head to toe in dirt. I can tell you now that being arrested and charged with drink driving and other traffic offences were the absolute least of his worries and he knew it. It turns out that the brand new Prelude he had been driving was not stolen as we first thought nor was it his. In fact it belonged to his wife who didn't even know he had it.

Now, I don't claim to be an expert in how women think or act.

Truthfully I have no idea. I just do as I'm told in an attempt to keep my head above water. This guy, in my opinion, was not just trying to tread water he was doing it with a Honda Prelude tied to his foot.

To really cap off the night he was having, a car pulled up and yes you guessed it she got out of the passenger seat still wearing her pyjamas. She didn't say a word. She looked at the car then walked straight over to where her husband was being breath tested and gave him one of the best right hooks I have ever seen. Her betrothed went straight down and said, 'Don't worry, I deserved that.' She was restrained because I was sure she wanted to literally lay the slipper into him. I've seen some angry women in my time and usually it's because of something I've done but this was the angriest lady I have ever seen. Her parting words were, 'I want him charged with stealing my car and I'm not going to bail him out, he can rot there.'

She was true to her word and had him charged. He pleaded guilty and probably had to leave the Central Coast to save his own life.

Ice

I would have to say that the drug commonly known as Ice is the greatest scourge on our society. This filthy drug gets people hooked after their first go then rapidly turns them from normal members of society into criminals totally obsessed with getting more no matter what the cost. It not only destroys the user, it destroys everyone around them as well. This story is from the time that Ice had just started to hit our streets.

It was about 3am in mid-winter Sydney when I heard a very shrill call for urgent assistance from a car crew working in the south western suburbs. I had just turned on to this area's channel and saw a General Duties truck come absolutely flying past me with its lights and sirens on. I went from bored to adrenalin-charged in a split second. I took off after the truck. I called police radio and told them I was on the way. They told me there were already three crews of two police at the scene and they were calling for urgent assistance. The original job was for a male acting suspiciously. Just after that there was another high-pitched call over the radio which I couldn't understand but I knew that these guys were in big trouble.

I pushed my car as fast as it would go, coming into the street in question at a great rate of knots. I could see what was happening but couldn't quite believe it.

There was one very muscular guy about 190cm tall with no shirt on and covered from head to toe in blood. He was punching and kicking the six police officers who were trying to subdue him. He punched one constable to her face and knocked her flat on her back, laughing as he did so. The other police had emptied six canisters of capsicum spray into his face which had absolutely no effect other than to make him even more aggressive. He was being struck with the full-size spun aluminium batons and again laughed every time he took a strike. There was police uniform and equipment lying all over the road. Most surprisingly, he was getting on top of the police; they were buggered and fast running out of options. One of them saw me and exclaimed, 'Thank God, get the dog over here quick.'

I got Merlin out and he immediately locked onto the crook. He was screaming, shouting and threatening to kill any pigs that came any closer. One of the police there shouted that the crook was on Ice and not feeling any pain whatsoever.

We got closer with Merlin barking and going mad at the surreal situation presented before us. At this stage all the police pulled back and waited for us to do something. I went to about 2m from the crook and shouted at him, 'Police, sit down and give up mate, you need an ambulance.' I was in no mood to go too near because of the huge amount of blood covering his body. He just turned towards us and with a look that reminded me of a cheap horror flick, hissed at me, 'Fuck you and your dog, I'll kill you.' Before I could reply he charged forward and started to swing his fists at me. Merlin went straight into action and clamped his jaws onto the crook's inner thigh. I had no choice but to retaliate in self-defence. I had let go of Merlin's lead and faced up to my attacker. I struck him with a closed fist to the side of his face and this, along with Merlin's help, sent him crashing to the ground. He looked straight back up at me and laughed, 'Is that all you've got?' He jumped up totally oblivious to Merlin and came at me again. By now his eyes were spinning at 1000 rpm and the stench of blood and capsicum spray was filling my senses. I was a bit worried because this drug-induced psychosis was all consuming and driving this bloke to extreme violence. There was only one thing for it so I dropped my shoulder and charged him. I hit him in the sweet spot under his ribs and up ended his crazed body. We both went to ground with Merlin growling and still hanging on to the same piece of flesh.

I yelled out to the other police to come over and pile on. They all rushed in and as one, six of them piled on. It was like watching an American baseball game when they win the World Series and jump the guy who hits the winning run. I got in close to Merlin's head and gave him a command. Even though there were bodies everywhere he had hung on to his quarry until I told him to stop. He spat the thigh out and we pulled back.

To my amazement, even with six police on him the crook was able to start getting up. I rushed back and put Merlin into the car then returned and jumped on the pile of bodies. It still took us another ten minutes of wrestling to get the handcuffs on and put his bloodied body in the back of a police truck. By the end of it we were all covered in his blood and exhausted. I had to sit down and take a few moments before I was able to get up. I just about took a bath in the antiseptic lotion we keep in our cars. Then, after going to hospital for blood tests, I went home. I had to wait for about six weeks before I knew I was clear from any blood contamination.

I heard that the next day the guy on Ice woke up in extreme agony in hospital under police guard and asked what had happened and how he got there. If you're ever tempted to try Ice then think of this story and walk away.

Two Plus One
Makes Three

It was about 9pm on a winter's evening when we were called to Toongabbie behind the shops in the CBD there. I arrived to find a red Commodore sedan parked under a block of units with three doors open and the engine running. The car had been chased by Blacktown Highway Patrol, lost for a short time (about two minutes) then located here in this condition. There had been a number of other cars involved in the chase and a good perimeter had been set around the entire area of the shops. The car was stolen and there was a computer sitting on the back seat. I asked the guys and they told me that they thought there were only two offenders in the vehicle but three of the doors were open. It can be quite hard to count passengers when you're screaming sideways around corners at mayhem speed trying to keep calm while you either drive or call the pursuit over the police radio.

I harnessed Merlin and started to track from the driver's door of the Commodore. He immediately gave me a very strong indication and was tracking very confidently along the asphalt. We tracked into the rear car park of a shop then up an alleyway that led to the rear entrance. He stopped at an outside laundry/toilet, put his paws on the windowsill and started barking. Too easy, I thought. I pulled Merlin back then put him in a heel position at my side. I yelled for whoever was inside to come out. Very slowly the door opened and I saw two very nervous males inside. They came out one at a time with their hands on their heads. Both were sweating heavily and, by the looks of them, knew what the inside of a gaol cell looked like.

By this time, the two highway officers had run up the alley to help. One of the offenders, who was quite large, started to mouth off at us and was resisting the highway guys who were trying to handcuff him. Merlin was going to have none of this and bucked and bounced as he tried to get in and help out the highway patrol. They got into a scuffle and eventually all three of them crashed to the ground in a melee of blue and white until the cuffs went on him. Meanwhile, the second runner who I was watching thought he was half a chance as he started to slowly sidle down the alley thinking I wasn't watching him. I told him not to bother as I would send the dog if he ran. He looked back at us and I could tell he was considering giving an escape attempt a go. I didn't know it at the time but he had a number of warrants out against him and knew he was going back to gaol for about two years. Just as he turned to run I reached out and grabbed his shoulder. This turned Merlin's attention away from the first crook and onto the second one. He assisted by grabbing his buttocks and trousers. He screamed in pain and fell to the ground pleading for the dog to let him go. I gave Merlin a command and he let go of the now-bruised buttocks. More police turned up and he was also cuffed and led away, walking in a bit of pain. 'Good boy,' I told Merlin who stuck his chest out, letting everybody know he was big and tough. I decided to get Merlin out of his tracking gear in the alley.

I was in the process of winding up his tracking line when he broke his sit and moved to the laundry door and started to growl. I thought he was picking up the residual scent that had been left by the first two runners. I called him back and put him in a heel position. I put on his normal lead and started to walk back, but Merlin wouldn't go. Again he walked back to the door and started to growl then bark. I had assumed that the other police had looked at this area. Never assume anything. I opened the door about 30cm when it was pushed into my face quite hard. So naturally I pushed back. I was pissed off because whoever was behind there hadn't missed and my face was now quite sore. I managed to get the door open about 50cm, which was enough for Merlin to shove his way in. All of a sudden the door went limp; I heard a cry of pain and Merlin's growl. I looked in and saw that he was dragging the last runner out by his left arm. As he was forced out, the crook had a swing at me with his right fist but missed, grabbing my overalls in an attempt to pull me down. I had to counter with a good hard strike on the shoulder with my torch which forced him to let go. He fell to the ground with Merlin still holding on to his arm. I called the other police who came running up and threw this last little Mike Tyson wannabee into the back of the police truck with the others. They all turned out to be well-known criminals with lengthy records. All three went back to where they needed to be, gaol.

Another Car Chase

This job has two parts to it. About 8pm on a winter's night, a call was put over the police radio about some young males in a red car acting suspiciously in a car park in Crows Nest on Sydney's Lower North Shore. I attended with a couple of cars from North Sydney Police. We found the car and four young men skulking around looking into cars. They tried to hide in a laneway when we turned up which made us all instantly suspicious. A check on each of them revealed that they were all known for stealing cars and were all from Bankstown, miles away. They said they were just trying to meet girls. I told them that was one of the worst excuses I had ever heard considering they were hanging around back alleys and laneways. Their car was searched and found to be full of things like jemmy bars, screwdrivers and other tools. Unfortunately there wasn't much we could do unless we caught them with the tools outside the car. The North Sydney boys took the details of all of them and told them to go home.

Not much else happened that night until about 3am when a call came over the radio that a member of the public was watching a male steal his Nissan Skyline GTS from his front yard in Frenchs Forest. Then a few minutes later it took off towards Warringah Road. At the time I was walking around the industrial area of Artarmon, which is about 10km from where this was happening. We ran back to the car and absolutely belted across towards the Roseville Bridge. I knew that if they were coming south then this was the only route they could take.

I turned onto Boundary Street at Roseville and slowed down hoping that I would see the Skyline coming the other way. Bingo, about ten seconds later I saw the Skyline driving in the opposite direction. I also saw a red car following very close behind. After a very fast U-turn I came up behind the red car which was, you guessed it, the same one from Crows Nest and it only had three people on board. I pulled out past them and slotted in behind the Skyline. I confirmed the registration with police radio; it was the stolen car.

About a kilometre from the Pacific Highway, the Skyline accelerated away in an attempt to lose me, and the pursuit was on. I switched on all the lights and sirens and came to a position about 50m behind the car. Pursuits become very busy, very fast when you're on your own. I had to drive the car, watch the offending vehicle, watch out for other traffic and pedestrians and call what was happening on the police radio. All this while Merlin is barking his head off in the back.

The police radio ask you a number of questions including the weather and road conditions, speed of offending vehicle, how heavy the traffic is, a constant update of your location, your driving experience and class of police licence and vehicle. You have to be able to take in all the information you're being bombarded with and give out all the information that the operators at police radio need while trying to sound calm and in control over the air. If you start screaming your tits off, it's very hard for anyone to know what's going on and how to best help.

Luckily for me, this thief wasn't much of a driver. He was in a GTS Skyline, which is a very powerful sports car. I was driving a Commodore station wagon. He should have been able to get away easily considering his horsepower and suspension advantage. I pursued him off Boundary Street and into the residential backstreets of Chatswood at speeds which varied from 80-120km/h. It's very exciting and frightening at the same time when you hit speed humps at those speeds. This went on for a short while until he came back out onto Boundary Street and turned right into Archbold Road. He then made another immediate turn into Margaret Street, fishtailing all over the road.

I followed him in and realised it was a dead-end road after he locked up his brakes, filling the whole street with smoke. I was expecting him to get out and run which would have been great. Merlin could have rounded him up in no time at all. Instead he flicked his car into reverse and rammed the front of mine. He smoked up his tyres and howled off in a u-turn back to the main road. I did exactly the same thing and chased him back towards the highway.

This guy had taken the pursuit to another much more dangerous level—he was obviously prepared to use any means whatsoever to get away even if it meant injuring or killing a police officer. By this time there were a number of other police cars involved. They all slotted in behind me as we chased him onto the Pacific Highway south towards the city at about 150km/h.

My car was fast running out of brakes due to the fast accelerating and braking which had taken place on the back streets. The thief was driving at around 100km/h when my two colleagues from Harbourside Highway Patrol turned up in their Silver V8 Falcon. Yes, the same two officers and car from the car jacking. They came past me and took over the chase. The observer gave me a 'not again' look as they accelerated past. This was a relief as I could now focus on driving and not calling the pursuit. We chased him to Crows Nest where he turned off the Pacific Highway and sped down a laneway going over humps and bottoming the car out which threw up massive amounts of sparks. It was like what you see when the world rally cars go flat out on narrow dirt roads in Europe, the only difference being that this was real. Our cars were getting the same treatment and it was only a matter of time before there was going to be an incident. As far as I was concerned and police radio allowed us (if this were the middle of the day with a lot of members of the public around we would have terminated the pursuit ourselves), there was no way we were going to let this one get away.

Unfortunately for him he was lost and had no idea where he was. But he was about to find out. He drove into the Mater Hospital at 100km/h straight into a massive fig tree, completely destroying the front end of the Skyline in a shower of glass and splitting metal. Thank God there was nobody about.

This Craig Lowndes wannabee still wasn't finished because, incredibly, he jumped out unscathed from the smoking wreck and took off on foot with the highway guys in close pursuit. He jumped off the side of a car park from two floors up and kept running. I was about 100m behind with Merlin dragging me the same way they had run. When we found them all, the two highway officers were wrestling with him on the car park floor. We raced in and the first thing I saw was the crook pulling out a screwdriver from his pocket. I thought he was going to use it to stab the highway officers so I intervened and released my grip on Merlin's lead just enough to allow him to bite the offending hand which immediately dropped the weapon.

He started to cry, giving in completely. I gave Merlin a command and he immediately let go of the crook's hand. We cuffed him and placed him in the back of a police truck.

I was not surprised to see his photo from earlier on in the night with one of the North Sydney police officers. At least we knew where we could find his mates. Just goes to show that you don't need a long neck to be one.

Get a Haircut & a Job

It was a very warm and muggy night in Sydney's west. In fact, we had just finished up a school search at Northmead; Merlin had worked hard in the heavy conditions to no avail. We had searched the buildings and tracked out a window and onto the street where we lost the scent. Most likely they had got away in a car. Anyway, Merlin had his face buried in his water bowl and as usual, he was noisy and making a mess of it, with water and slobber flying in all directions.

I was just finishing packing his tracking gear away when the silence was broken by the police radio. 'Parramatta 41 urgent, in foot pursuit.' My ears pricked up and I got that little shot of adrenalin.

Foot pursuits are one of our favourite things. The beat crew calling the foot pursuit had disturbed a male breaking into cars out the front of a block of units in Parramatta. I was literally two minutes away and set off with the lights on and sirens screaming. The call came over to go to a back street where they had lost the runner just near a block of units. They stayed where they were and didn't have to wait long for us to arrive.

I spoke to the police who were still literally getting their breath back. They said that he had only been 20m in front when he rounded the corner. They turned the same corner seconds later and he was gone.

I opened up the back of the car and put a still-panting Merlin on his lead. He came over to where I harnessed him up at about half speed, not what you'd call energetic. I was just about to harness him up when his whole persona changed; he became completely alert with his ears and tail going straight up. He started to whine and indicate towards the driveway of the first block of units which led underground. I kept him on his lead while he dragged me straight down the driveway to the entrance of the underground car park. At the time, there were only four to five cars inside with room for about thirty more. Along one of the walls was a large pile of rubbish including an old sofa and fridge. The only way out was back through the car park entrance or through a secure internal door which led into the unit block itself. Merlin was trying to get free of his lead and starting to growl and salivate. I yelled out, 'Police, come out or I'll send the dog.' No response. I gave the challenge again and again there was no response. Merlin was barking and jumping around in excitement, and it wasn't fair to hold him back any longer. Well, he's had every chance to give himself up, I thought. I gave Merlin a command and let him go.

He launched off with his hind legs and started to search the car park bouncing back and forth like a hairy pinball. The police officers with me wanted to go in and help, but I stood in front and said, 'Just wait here boys and let him use his gift.' It wasn't long and Merlin was starting to hone in on the origin of the scent. He checked under every car and looked in every shadowy corner. His searching pattern became smaller and smaller until he came to the pile of household rubbish sitting up against the wall. I told him he was a good boy as I saw him hackle up his back and puff out his chest. He jumped up on an old lounge and started to bark whilst jumping up and down trampoline style. I ran up and yelled out, 'Police, come out now, I know you're under there.' There was no response at all. Merlin decided that this was going nowhere and took matters into his own hands, so to speak. He went to the side of the rubbish pile and stuck his nose between the old lounge and wall. He had stopped barking and was now letting out his low growl. I knew the crook was in there but couldn't see exactly where. I wasn't going to start poking around to possibly be stabbed or injured by some other kind of weapon. This guy wasn't prepared to come out on his own so it was time to help Merlin make him come out. I jumped in next to Merlin and pulled on the lounge as hard as I could. With all the weight on top and around it I was only able to drag the entire thing about 15cm further off the wall. I was about to give it a second effort when I glanced down and saw that Merlin had his entire head in the gap and had a hold of something in his mouth. He was pig rooting it back through the gap, but I still couldn't see what it was until I heard a call for help from under the lounge.

Merlin had got hold of the crook's large plaited pigtail and was dragging him out from his hiding place by it. I gave him a 'good boy' as the 100kg crook was dragged fully out with both his hands grabbing onto his end of the pigtail. It didn't do him any good as there was no way Merlin was letting go until I told him to. The crook kept trying to get up and even had a few swings at me and Merlin. But Merlin was too strong and just kept dragging him down every time he tried to break free. The other police came over and put on the handcuffs while I gave Merlin his command, making him let go of the now unravelled pigtail.

After putting Merlin back in the car with another messy bowl of water, I went back over to where the crook was seated. He complained that he was just trying to make a living and no one was really getting hurt. Like I said, 'Get a hair cut and a real job.'

A Country Trip

One of the things you get to do in the Dog Squad is travel to country New South Wales and assist the police out there. Rural policing is quite different to big city policing. I found it strange at first that most people in the bush will come up and say hello. I suppose I've been in the city too long and am too used to people staring or being rude. Things run a lot slower and it's actually quite relaxing; even while you're working there just isn't the same ugly buzz that is a constant in the city. That having been said, there are still a few things that never change even though they're on a much smaller scale.

I had made the trip to the central western town of Coonabarabran at the end of summer. This region was in the grip of a very long and hard drought. The difference between the coastal areas of New South Wales and Central New South Wales is dramatic and much worse than I had imagined. More than once I had to pull over and wait till a dust storm cleared due to poor visibility. When I arrived I was warmly welcomed by the local police who had set up the old exercise and cell complex in the station as a kennel. Merlin's accommodation was set and he would be much happier in there than in the back of the car as would normally be the case. There was a rodeo and show in town and I was going to assist the local police with keeping the peace. Some years

117

the alcohol has flowed a bit too freely and all the mayhem of running battles with the police has been seen down the main street of town. If this were the case again then Merlin and I would be more than willing to help out. Most of the night went without incident. The local crooks and troublemakers in town knew that there were larger than normal numbers of police in town along with a rather large police dog. As part of our duties, we had to patrol the car park on foot. The only thing we found there apart from passed out drunks were a couple of teenagers in the back of a ute fumbling with each other's clothes. The look on their faces was priceless when Merlin jumped up onto the side of the ute and started to bark. If it was their first time then I doubt either will ever forget it. I said hello and told them to have a good night, then kept on walking. I didn't want to be known as the fun police.

Of course, no event where alcohol is served would be complete without an obnoxious and abusive drunk. It was about half an hour after the show had stopped and the last of the drinkers were leaving. I was standing out the front of the showground choking on the dust being thrown up by vehicles when this bloke who had been standing on the opposite corner of the street stumbled over to a highway patrol car and used probably every swear word I've ever heard to describe the officers and their families. He capped it off by kicking in a patrol car's quarter panels. Having a good sense of humour is one thing but the line has to be drawn somewhere. This bloke had just stepped right over that line and put his boot into it. The two officers jumped out of their vehicle and approached the offending drunk who turned and ran like a rabbit.

It's about time, I thought. We took off after him along with one of the highway patrol officers. I kept Merlin on lead as there were a lot of cars still around and even police dogs have a brain the size of a pea when it comes to road sense. Luckily this drunk jumped into the local bowling club. We followed him over and I heard him jumping fences about 50m in front of us. This area was very quiet so I gave Merlin a command and sent him off to find the drunk. Now I might add that because of the numerous run-ins that we have had with drunks, Merlin dislikes the smell of alcohol on a person. If I've had a night out on the drink and come home to feed him he still to this day has a little growl at me when I put down his bowl of food.

Merlin disappeared into the darkness and started to search. He cleared the bowling club then ran out into the street beside the greens. I watched him start to get excited as he hackled up and puffed out his chest. He had picked something up. He ran back along the street with a real look of purpose then into the darkness at the end. About thirty seconds later I heard him start to bark. When I ran down to where he was standing I saw a 3m-high Colorbond fence, which ran around a house at the end of the cul-de-sac. I knew that whoever he was chasing had run into there. The gate had been left unlocked so all I had to do was push it open while Merlin ran past me into the yard and continued on searching. He ran down the side of the house on the opposite end of the yard and started to bark about two seconds later. I lit it up with the torch and saw the drunk lying on his back kicking out at Merlin who now had hold of his jeans and was dragging him out to me. What I saw made me take a step back. The drunk's arm and clothing were saturated with blood and the fence and side of the house were covered with blood. All I could think was how the hell did Merlin do that to him in such a short space of time? It's just not possible.

I called Merlin off and had a closer look at the screaming offender's arm. The blood was coming from a cut to his thumb. By cut I mean that it was sliced to the bone and had almost taken the whole thing off. As it turned out he had jumped the Colorbond fence but had not noticed that there was no cap over the top. He had put all his body weight on the top of the fence that was razor sharp aluminium, almost cutting off his thumb. He was taken to the local hospital where they took one look then sent him to Dubbo hospital for microsurgery.

Being a small town the word had got around about this incident. So by the time the story got back to me the consensus around town was that Merlin had caught the drunk and ripped his thumb completely off his hand in a savage, unbridled attack. I had retrieved the pieces and sent them to hospital in Dubbo to have them re-attached. This had a very positive result because that night, which was the last of the show, was very quiet and there wasn't a soul in town after closing time. By 1am there was really nothing for any of us to do. All the pubs were so quiet that they shut early. For the first time in a long time, there was nowhere to get a drink in town on a weekend night. I do love getting out into the fresh country air.

The Running of the Bulls

It was 4am on a very cold morning and we had been called out to a semi-rural suburb of western Sydney. There had been a car chase with the driver of the stolen vehicle caught at the scene and the passenger disappearing into a paddock. I had arrived about twenty minutes later and started a track. I had a probationary constable come along, as I was totally unfamiliar with this part of Sydney.

The track started well and travelled through a number of paddocks then into long grass. I could see where this offender had taken a breather, hollowing out parts of the paddock. We finally went into a paddock where Merlin suddenly stopped and lifted up his head; he was wind scenting something. I tried to see without using the torch but it was way too dark. I turned it on and saw about twenty pairs of eyes shining in the dark. All of a sudden they started to move in our direction. I still couldn't see what they were attached to as they came closer and closer until I saw bulls with horns. They weren't walking, they were trotting and fast approaching us. I turned to the probationer and asked her if she was a fast runner. She asked why so I shone the torch back on the charging bulls. Before I could say, 'That's why', she was gone, running back towards the fence.

I turned with every intention of running away and jumping to the safe side of the barrier, but Merlin had other ideas. He wanted to mount a last stand or banzai charge back at the herd of charging bovines. I had to scream 'No!' and drag him back towards safety. I managed to throw him over the barbed wire then flung myself after him. I had to just lie there and catch my breath before I could drag myself up. Luckily the only injuries I received were a few cuts to my legs and torn overalls. The herd of bulls charged right up to the wire fence snorting and steaming in the cool night air. I'm sure they would have happily gored or trampled us to death if Merlin had done things his way. I turned to walk away but had to look back and say, 'Hopefully the next time I see you lot will be on my barbecue while I enjoy a beer.' I wasn't game to try and get to where the track continued—it just wasn't worth dying over, so we returned and left the job at that. At least the driver had been caught and I was in one piece no thanks to Mr Suicide.

Help Me Mummy

I had just returned from a trip to South Africa. Merlin had been looked after in the police kennels at Menai while I was away and was glad to be out and about again with me in the car. When I went to pick him up, one of the kennel attendants opened his kennel door and he just about knocked me down and licked me to death. He dragged me straight out to the car and jumped in the back as if to say, 'Come on Dad, let's go!'

It was the first hour of our first shift back on a summer afternoon. I was happy to be back and it didn't take long for our services to be required. A Gladesville car had been sent to the ferry wharf at Meadowbank after a report of about twenty males in cars intimidating and threatening people as they left the wharf. There were only six police officers in attendance and they were struggling to move along the group which outnumbered them four to one. As usual, with people like this they are very tough, hard individuals in a group but a pack of soft little ballet girls when the odds are less than in their favour. Merlin and I were about to even things up for the police team.

I had not been far from the scene when the call for assistance came over the radio. I pulled in and saw a group of males of middle-eastern background standing in front and around the side of the six police officers who were involved in an argument with them. There were also a number of ridiculously modified cars parked in such a way that they were stopping everyone else from using the parking facilities. I opened up the back of my car and put Merlin onto his lead. I was staring at the group who were still unaware of my presence, unlike the police who had seen me turn up. The group of males were mouthing off and basically telling the police officers to 'piss off and leave us alone.' I didn't say a word—I didn't have to as Merlin already had them targeted and was hackled up in anticipation. I walked around the trouble makers, some of whom had by now noticed our presence and had stopped talking. Very soon the whole group had gone silent and were watching as we came up beside the police. I turned to the nearest officer and asked whether these people had been directed to move along from this area. She said they had and that they wanted to arrest two of them for assault, pointing out two of these heroes who were standing up against a wall trying to act tough. Merlin was just staring at them, watching every movement they made. Just as the constable had finished explaining the situation to me, one of the group came towards us and said, 'You don't understand, you can't tell us what to do.' He came straight at us and to save him from Merlin who I had on a very short, tight lead, I pushed him back and knocked him to the ground. I said, 'No, it's you that doesn't understand.' Merlin had launched at him to defend me and the only thing which saved him from a dog bite was my push in his chest. From then it was on. The police now had the upper hand and the cowardly group was backing away and trying to scurry into their cars. I made a beeline for the two crooks who were to be arrested for assault. They were trying to walk away but Merlin soon convinced them to stay put while two police handcuffed them and took away their liberty.

I turned to see two of the group get into one of their cars. They had been parked in by one of the police vehicles and were sounding their horn. The driver stuck his head out the window and yelled, 'Move the fucking pig mobile.' I walked over and said, 'Would you like to repeat yourself?' He looked at me and shouted, 'Fuck off or I'll run you down.' Merlin had picked up on the aggression so he put his paws up on the door and stuck his head in the window, letting loose with a barrage of barking, growling and dog slobber which made the driver back away onto his passenger's lap. I told the driver to get out as he was under arrest for that language. Instead, he gunned the engine and drove away because the police car had unwittingly been moved by one of the other police so they could load in their prisoners. Both Merlin and I had to jump away to avoid being dragged by the car. I memorised the number plate as the driver gave me 'the bird' and accelerated out of the car park and up the hill. The rest of the rabble had run away and order had been restored so that people could now use the ferry and car park without being harassed and assaulted.

I checked the rego I had memorised over the police radio. The operator told me that the car was registered to an address which was only about 500m from the ferry wharf. I gathered the police and put a panting Merlin back into the car. We all drove up the road to the address and bingo, the car was parked out the front.

I hadn't even got out of the car when the front door of the house opened and a middle-aged woman came out with the driver walking behind her. He yelled, 'That's the one, Mama, he threatened me.'

I got out and walked straight over to them. I informed him that he was under arrest for offensive language and assaulting police. To my surprise, the alleged 'man' hid behind his mother and said, 'You can't do that—this is my mum.' I laughed and asked him if he was really going to use his mummy to hide from the police. She told me that her son was a good boy and that I couldn't take him. I told her I was sorry but her son was under arrest and I was going to take him. I grabbed hold of his arm and walked him back over to the other police who put him in the back of their truck with the other two already under arrest. I still can't believe that a twenty-three-year-old would use his mummy as a shield from the police in a bid to hide from the responsibilities of his actions. If Merlin could talk, I'm sure he'd shake his head in disgust as well.

You Don't Need a Long Neck To Be One

This thief really needs to do his homework if he expects to get away with crime on the North Shore of Sydney. This mental giant and his mate came from the far western suburbs of Sydney. They decided to break into vehicles and steal whatever they could find on the affluent North Shore. They started at 5pm in Kirribilli in the same street that the Prime Minister and his family reside in. Tensions in the Gulf were starting to get high, with Australia deploying troops; we were also coming to grips with the cowardly Bali bombing some months earlier. Security in this part of Sydney in particular was very high.

So, after two cars had been broken into, the Protective Services Officers who patrol the area chased the two thieves, tackling one right outside the front gates of Kirribilli House. The other one disappeared. I got there as fast as I could and started to search backyards and streets. I couldn't find anything and the other thief wasn't saying anything. After about an hour of looking I decided to call it quits and have some dinner, and as I was down by the water on the most beautiful harbour in the world I decided to dine there and then. I had just finished eating when a lady walked up to me and told me that a male with no shirt on, covered in tattoos with a shaved head had come out of the water, seen me, turned around and run back along the foreshore towards the Prime Minister's house.

I thanked her and got Merlin out. I trotted over to where she had last seen him and started to track. Merlin tracked very hard and I knew that he wasn't very far ahead. Unfortunately I had a full stomach and running in my bloated condition was uncomfortable to say the least. We tracked over fences and around the foreshore along the water east back towards Kirribilli House. I called on the police radio and told them what was happening. About a minute later I heard a message over the radio that a male fitting the same description had been caught inside the Prime Minister's grounds by security staff.

I tracked on and came to the fence at the side of Kirribilli House. Over we went. I knew that we had just set off a number of alarms and sensors but they knew I was coming. I was met by one of the officers who told me that the offender had already been arrested and placed in custody inside the grounds. I tracked to a gazebo where the track stopped. He confirmed that this is where the brain surgeon had been ambushed and arrested. They had tracked him with their security devices as soon as he entered the grounds. Yeah, that was a really well thought out escape route, you master criminal you. Both were charged with offences relating to breaking into and stealing from cars. The second was also charged with offences relating to entering the Prime Minister's residence.

World's Shortest Catches

Sometimes to track an offender you have to go kilometres over fences, through yards, down streets and through creeks. Tracking is an art that takes a lot of time and there are numerous challenges to master. After four years of tracking, I still make mistakes and am constantly trying to improve on what I have already learnt.

On this particular evening in Sydney's north I was called to the home of a mentally ill youth who had attacked his family and threatened them with a knife. As I walked through their house and into the backyard I could tell that they had had enough and were at the end of their tether. The inside of the house looked as if it had been involved in a wild west saloon brawl. There was broken furniture and glass everywhere. The mentally ill guy's mother was collapsed on a lounge crying while her two other children tried to comfort her. His father was at the back door and looked like a beaten man. He pointed out the back door and said, 'He went that way.' I peered out and saw that the yard had a tennis court in it with a small, grassed area that contained a shed at the rear. The boy had been last seen running into the tennis court, then he disappeared. He needed to be medicated and there were genuine fears that he may hurt someone if he wasn't found soon. Obviously he wasn't in the tennis court so I harnessed Merlin into his tracking gear at the rear gate of the court. He was already getting excited jumping around and making it hard for me to fit on his harness. I had an idea that the young bloke was quite near.

I gave Merlin his command and he started searching the ground for scent. Soon he focussed and started to track. I hadn't even started to move my feet when he stopped at the front of the shed and started to bark. I had only let out about five feet of tracking line! There was nowhere else to hide so I opened up the rusty door and lit up the interior. Sure enough, the subject of our search was hiding inside. He was scared out of his mind, and he wailed and screamed in terror. I pulled Merlin back and called the general duties police over so they could bring him out. Merlin's imposing presence wasn't doing anyone any favours. We were able to get the young bloke the care and attention that he needed.

That last catch was for a relatively minor matter however this next one was also a short-distance catch, but involved the arrest of an extremely violent and dangerous armed robber. I was on day shift and had gone down to our base at Menai to complete some paperwork. I didn't mind being inside on this particular day as it had been raining for a week and was still coming down in bucket loads—the police and tow truck drivers had been busier than a one-armed brick layer in Baghdad.

I heard a call for a dog to go to North Sydney in relation to an armed offender who they believed was hiding somewhere in the North Sydney CBD. I was a bit sceptical, as I know there is a huge amount of pedestrian traffic in this area. I got on the air and told them I was on the way. It's about 45–50km to North Sydney from Menai and it was raining. I turned on the lights and sirens and managed to get there in good time, which was quite surprising considering the conditions and the fact that a lot of people on the roads don't seem to be able to move out of the way to the left when you are coming through! (I bet they'd move if I was going to catch someone who was breaking into their house or belting someone they care about.)

When I arrived in Mount Street, I spoke to an inspector who told me that about 40 minutes earlier this offender, who had done about thirty armed hold-ups in the last month with his girlfriend, had been seen by two uniformed police. They had approached them and tried to place the pair under arrest. A scuffle broke out which resulted in this criminal pulling out an automatic pistol from under his shirt. This is especially frightening not only because there was a good chance the crook may shoot the police, but also that where it happened was a very busy street and using a police fire arm to defend yourself could result in civilian casualties. Luckily one of the constables managed to hit the gun out of his hand. If he hadn't done this and a gun fight had started then there would definitely have been a huge amount of casualties among bystanders. Unfortunately the gun fell to the ground at the feet of this grub's girlfriend, so the police had to arrest her and secure the firearm. Meanwhile, he ran off down the street minus his shirt, which had been ripped off during the struggle. One of the police gave chase but lost him among the twists and turns of Little Walker Street.

Luckily again for the police, there was a highway patrol enforcement on in the area and a dozen of these officers were able to get on the scene within minutes and form a perimeter. Even luckier was the fact that there were about thirty police officers on a training day at North Sydney Police Station who immediately came down to the scene to make the perimeter even stronger.

I was speaking to this inspector on the corner of Mount Street and Little Walker Street. I thought that if the crook was going to be anywhere it was one of the car parks down Little Walker Street. I got out Merlin and started to walk along the side of one of the buildings. This was still going to be hard because there were members of the public walking inside the car parks and along the street. We had walked no more than 20m when Merlin started to drag me into a double car space in an alcove under a high rise. He hackled up and started to wag his tail in that 'I've found someone' fashion of his. The space was empty except for a large wheelie bin at the rear. We went up to it and Merlin started to growl. I looked over the rear of the bin with my torch and bingo, there he was—our runner minus his shirt squatting down in the garbage with his face in his hands.

Merlin was by now going berserk, barking and salivating at the unseen body emanating the scent. I shouted to the offender, 'Police, come out hands first and give up.' Both his hands came up from behind the bin followed by his dejected face. He took one look at Merlin, swore and climbed out. He kept his hands in the air and stumbled out without so much as a whimper. He was arrested by about twenty police officers who had swarmed to the entrance of the car park. He was handcuffed and taken back to North Sydney Police Station where he was interviewed then charged with all his armed robbery offences plus a few more relating to firearms and trying to use them on police. This was a very short but very sweet arrest by Merlin. Dog handlers love to catch armed robbers as they are generally at the top of the most desired offence hit list. This armed robber is on his way to Long Bay where he belongs, thanks to the hairy one and his all-star nose.

With a dog as good as Merlin it's too easy sometimes to take his talents for granted. I have to constantly remind myself that even the most simple of searches and arrests don't just happen through good luck and favourable circumstances. They happen because we work as a team. Through constant hard work in training and operational work, Merlin is able to make it look simple. We turned up to a Break and Enter at a restaurant in The Rocks area of Sydney. I rolled up and saw the police standing out the front next to a broken glass window. The restaurant consisted of a bar and dance floor with tables around the edge. All up it wasn't a particularly large area. They told me that the alarm had gone off about half an hour before I arrived and about fifteen minutes before they had arrived. I didn't think there was much hope of finding anyone still inside but since the local guys had done the right thing and waited outside until I could search, I collected Merlin and went in. I was already planning on putting one of the police officers inside after we had finished so that we could do some training. I have to admit that I probably didn't sound too convincing when I issued my verbal challenge to the inside of the restaurant. Merlin barked and as usual he charged in and started to search with enthusiasm. I watched him but stayed just inside the door trying to locate a good hiding spot for one of the officers. Then I got the kick up the rear I deserved for being complacent. It had only been about one minute and Merlin was at a rear folding door barking. I thought, 'You've got to be kidding.'

Sure enough, as I side stepped and swerved my way to the back of the table seating, I saw Merlin trying to push the folding door in with his front legs while getting his head through the gap he had opened. All the time he was barking and growling at whoever was trying to push the door shut. I gave him a huge and heartfelt 'good boy', a little disgusted at myself for not being as switched on and professional as he was. I managed to get his head out of the gap and put him on his lead. I yelled out, 'Police, come out with your hands showing and give up.' I immediately got a reply, 'Okay, okay, I'm coming, just keep that dog away from me.' Slowly the door opened and a pair of gloved hands appeared, followed by a crook who was completely dressed in black from head to toe. He still had on his balaclava with only holes for his eyes. Merlin went crazy at this apparition; the more bizarre a bad guy looks then the greater the drive becomes in the dog. This crook was marched out and arrested. It turns out he had watched one too many movies and was trying to go through the wall of the restaurant and into the bank next door! We found cutting tools and the start of a hole this clown had put in the wall. I think he had forgotten that it's not only banks that have alarms but restaurants as well.

I got a wake-up call too—never ever assume that nothing is going to happen and nobody is going to be there. Thanks Merlin.

The last short catch was in the middle of winter. I was enjoying a hot coffee while Merlin was enjoying a nap in the back of the car which was nice and warm compared to the freezing weather outside. I heard one of the Ku-ring-gai Highway patrol crews call a pursuit of a car which had run a random breath testing site and disappeared down a back alley in Gordon just off the Pacific Highway. I was at Chatswood, so I dumped the coffee and jumped back into the car. I gave the car a bit of hustle as the call came back that the car was stolen and had been dumped in an alleyway behind a car dealer. There were five or six highway patrol cars on the scene and a good perimeter had been established. Merlin sat up and shook his head as I rudely interrupted his slumber with the lights and sirens and 'urgent duty' driving.

It took us about three minutes to make it to the alleyway and the stolen car. The area is set just off the Pacific Highway and is entirely industrial with car yards, warehouses and office blocks. It was midnight and there was no one else around. I collected a now fully awake and alert Merlin from the car and put him in his tracking harness. He was jumping up and down and whining. The crook wasn't far ahead and Merlin could smell blood in the water. We started at the driver side door of the stolen Commodore; Merlin put his nose down and almost pulled my arms from the sockets when he took off tracking. He powered up the alleyway going half way up a number of driveways then back on to the alley. This was showing me that the driver was looking for somewhere to hide and was probably panicking as he heard the police sirens surround him. We had gone about 100m when Merlin stopped and lifted his head towards a raised garden full of low, thick shrubs. He put his nose back down but kept lifting to smell whoever it was on the wind. He jumped up the retaining wall and started to wag his tail. He charged in before I could get up the wall. The tracking line was very taut as he mowed through the shrubs then suddenly went slack. Merlin growled and started to bark. We had him. I climbed to the top of the retaining wall just in time to see Merlin cop a boot to his face. He recoiled then instantly dived back into the shrubs disappearing from my sight. I yelled out, 'Police, stop what you're doing and stand up.' I started to pull on the tracking line in an effort to get Merlin out of there. I didn't want him stabbed or otherwise seriously injured by this thief who I couldn't see even with the torch on. I should have had more faith as Merlin came out of the shrubs backwards, pig rooting the runner whose leg Merlin had firmly held in his mouth. I called in the highway officers who handcuffed the crook while I released him from Merlin's grip. I was a little annoyed to see that the crook's boot had connected with Merlin's nose making it bleed. He, on the other hand, had five stitches waiting for him at hospital so I'd say we could call that one even.

The Cliff Hanger

The crook in this story was pretty desperate to get away and deserves a mention for his sheer determination. His problem was that dog teams are usually more determined than the crooks to get a catch and make the arrest.

Again we were working on a weekend night with all the usual drunken violence that goes with it. We were called to a small wharf in Balmain where a man had been robbed of his wallet by a group of young males, then stabbed in the arm for his trouble. He had given a pretty good description of two of them who had been chased by local residents into a block of units. I decided to start there even though it had happened half an hour earlier. I didn't really think that we were going to get anyone because of that timeframe and the number of people out and about on foot at this time of the evening.

Merlin jumped out as usual full of beans and ready to roll. His enthusiasm is kind of infectious and I was running off his energy, perking up with a new determination to get a result for the victim. We went through the side gate of the old sandstone unit block and immediately Merlin pumped his rear legs and started to drag me towards a cyclone wire fence topped with barbed wire on the other side of the yard. I kept him on lead just in case it was an innocent member of the public and not our crooks. Merlin dragged me to a point in the fence where there was a low hedge and he barked, blocking up against the fence with his front paws. At that exact same moment a body sprung up from the hedge and legged it away. It was one of the crooks that had been described by the victim and witnesses. One of the main features was a white hoodie-style jumper with red and black writing on the front and back. This guy had that, along with blood stains on one of the sleeves. More worrying was the fact that he was carrying a small knife in one of his hands which thankfully he dropped when I yelled, 'Police, stop or I'll send the dog.'

Merlin was barking and champing at the bit to chase this runner down. Unfortunately there was no way over the fence because of the barbed wire and no way through as there was no gate. We sprinted for the front of the units, turning left out the front then left again into a very narrow residential street. In the sprint to the front I had dropped Merlin's tracking gear and didn't have time to go back and look for it. I trusted Merlin and followed him as he dragged me along with the lead. I decided that if we were going to get this guy then Merlin would be more efficient off his lead. I yelled a command and slipped him off. Merlin raced out ahead and took a corner, heading down towards the water. I soon lost sight of him and just kept on going in the last direction that he had gone. I figured that if the crook doubled back then Merlin would get him easily and it wouldn't be too far from where I was now. If he kept on going he would run out of land as the harbour was only 200m away.

About five to six minutes later, I heard Merlin barking from the direction of the water. It was faint but definitely my partner. I strode out in an effort to get there as soon as possible. Merlin did his job to perfection; he kept on barking and stayed with whoever he had found. This made it very easy for me to zero in on where they were. I had to climb the fence of a building site, negotiating the piles of bricks and debris scattered throughout. When I reached the far side closest to Merlin's bark I pulled up quickly, almost running straight off the edge of a drop and into the dark abyss below. I could hear that Merlin was down the cliff somewhere close and still operating. He definitely wasn't in distress; I could tell by the sound of his barking. I yelled out, 'Good boy, I'll be there in a sec.' I used the torch which illuminated a very narrow dirt track that ran along the side of the cliff face and the harbour 5–6m below. The track led off out of sight around a corner towards Merlin's barking.

There was only one thing for it. I bolted back through the building site and out onto the road again. I ran back towards a laneway I had seen on the way, hoping that it would get me down to the sea wall. Otherwise I was going to have to scale the cliff down to the track. I wasn't too keen on leaving Merlin down there for too much longer. Bingo, there it was, I sprinted along the track until it became so narrow I had to edge along it with my back to the seawall. It was a further 2m to the water and, as sweaty as I was, I did not feel like a swim.

I crabbed around the corner and, much to my relief, I came up behind Merlin who was sitting down on the track with his right-hand side pushed up against the cliff. He was still barking and only stopped for a short while to check out who was coming up behind him. Much to my amusement was the predicament of the criminal. He was about a metre and a half from the end of the track where Merlin was seated. He was clinging precariously to the cliff face and sweating from both running and nerves. I put Merlin back on his lead and told him he was a very good boy. I had called our position over police radio and could hear the sirens coming our way. The crook was too scared to come back. He told me he had jumped to where he was when he had heard Merlin's panting and growling voice come up behind him. By now the water police had arrived and lit up the area with a floodlight. I told him that he had three options: jump back over to the track; jump into the water and swim to the water police; or climb up the 4–5m to the top of the cliff to be met by the general duties police who had arrived. I told him that in my opinion he wasn't going to be able to hold on for much longer and would have to make a decision soon.

He opted for choice number one. I walked Merlin back around the corner and put him in a sit. He waited dutifully while I went back around and, using a borrowed police baton, reached out and hauled the crook back onto the track. He was so buggered by now that I just took hold of the back of his hoodie and escorted him back to where he was taken into custody by the waiting police. He got the evil eye and a little growl from Merlin as we passed, but he didn't break his sit. The crook ended up pleading guilty to malicious wounding and did some good time in gaol for his efforts.

Five-star Comfort

Usually when we travel to a country town, we stay at a local motel. It was mid-winter and we had been sent to Armidale, which is a very cold and miserable place when you're walking around on night shift. The local police were having trouble with drunken hoodlums in the centre of town on weekends. We were despatched to go and help them out on a street safe operation.

The temperature with wind chill factor included was about -5 degrees Celsius. I was wearing just about everything with which I had been issued and I was still freezing. I walked around cursing my own stupidity for volunteering to come. To make it worse, the local guys used to this weather were walking around like they were on the beachfront at Bondi in mid-summer. We had a few small issues with local hoodlums who, full of booze and bad manners, had their attitudes adjusted by Merlin who like the locals seemed to be enjoying the cold. One pair of booze hounds had seen us and made a beeline straight for us. But due to their level of intoxication they were talking at the tops of their voices as they approached. Drunk One said to his mate, 'I'll take the dog, you take the copper.' Drunk Two replied, 'No worries, I'll king hit him and we'll take his wallet.'

At first I thought they were joking but it became quite apparent they were serious. They both started to come in at a fast pace with fists clenched. I looked down at Merlin who was watching them intently and sensing that something was about to happen. I said in a very loud voice, trying to mimic these two Dutch courage heroes, 'Hey Merl, you take the one on the left and I'll take the one the right, and after hospital they can spend the night in the cells.' Merlin started to bark and pull hard in their direction, growling, salivating and pumping out his chest. Both these two had probably the only moment of clarity in their evening and stopped in their tracks. I said to them, 'Is there anything I can help you with?' The only answer was, 'No, we just wanted to pat your dog.' By this time the local boys were with us and they put these two in a police truck and took them home before they could get into any real trouble.

The rest of the night was relatively quiet and we returned to the motel. It was a Motor Inn and I parked the police car up in front of my room door. It was about 4am and absolutely bloody freezing. There was ice forming on the windows and roof of the car. I felt sorry for Merlin and let him inside my beautifully warm room. I put him on his mat beside my bed and we both went to sleep. I woke about 10am and looked down to find an empty mat beside the bed. No worries, I thought, he's in here somewhere. I looked around but there was no dog on the floor or in the bathroom! Where the hell is he? Then I heard a snore and satisfied snort come from the single bed next to my double. I had my bags and equipment stacked on top of this bed, so all I saw was a pair of hind legs sticking up from behind my gear. On closer inspection there was Merlin lying on his back, legs in the air and sound asleep in apparent five-star dog luxury. You smart little bugger, I thought. You're not stupid enough to try getting into my bed, no, you got into the empty one for a great night's sleep. You have to give him credit for that—he's not stupid.

Bash on Through

We were on a night shift and were out patrolling Westmead in the western suburbs of Sydney. There was a stolen car whose occupants had been breaking into cars and stealing car radios. There were about five local police cars and myself looking, and it was about 1am. This stolen Camry had just been seen prowling around the children's hospital about five minutes earlier. I was just starting to lose hope of finding them when the police radio burst into life, 'Parramatta 15 urgent, we've found that vehicle behind a block of units, the occupants have run off into the unit blocks, there's two of them.' About ten seconds later the police from Parramatta 15 had tackled one of the runners and taken him into custody. The second runner had taken off into the dark. The area was about three blocks of five to six unit buildings, all divided by fences and a number of labyrinth-like alleys. I was there in about two minutes. The local guys showed me where they had last seen the thief running, which was down a short alley and over a fence.

I harnessed Merlin into his tracking gear and gave him his command to start tracking. He was very excited and champing at the bit; this guy was close and he knew it. Merlin put his nose down and just about pulled my arms from their sockets. He came to the first fence and vaulted over like some kind of Olympian. I had no choice other

142

than to hang on for dear life, moving as fast as I could. We tracked through a couple of car parks and over a fence, continuing on through an alley. Merlin was so focused he didn't miss a beat and had his nose millimetres from the ground sucking in the offender's scent like a Hoover. About 2m from a wooden fence he started to growl; we were very close. I expected Merlin to jump this fence which was missing a few palings and about 2m high, easy. As it turned out, the thief was just on the other side trying to hide his breaking tools and a bag of stolen car radios. The next thing he knew, a black-and-tan freight train burst through the rotten timber fence in a shower of splinters and falling debris. Soon followed by his handler who was just along for the ride. I can still see the complete look of horror and fear as we ran straight over the top of him and his ill-gotten gains. He lay on the ground, put his hands behind his back as if to be handcuffed and said, 'Jesus Christ, I give up.'

The local cops were very happy—they had been after these crooks for a couple of weeks and were able to link them to a huge number of similar offences committed in the same area. Contrary to what some people think, frontline police are keen to catch the crooks and put them before the courts. This is not always easy and unlike TV crimes, cannot always be solved within the space of an hour. Your local police are generally hardworking and keen to solve crime, they just cannot be everywhere all the time.

So Near But So Far

This story starts with a very boring and hot day shift. There was nothing happening and it was high summer in Sydney. I was driving through Lidcombe in Sydney's west wishing I was at the beach when a call came over the police radio about a Break and Enter occurring now in Lidcombe. I pulled over and saw that the street where this was occurring was only about a kilometre from where I was. There was a neighbour watching; he was on the phone directly to the police radio operator who was feeding live updates to us directly over the police radio. There were three crooks who were still inside the house. A few seconds later one of the local highway patrol cars called off there. They knew I was close by so they snuck into the garden of the house and started to watch the thieves going about their business. They were able to see them through some large glass doors and could give a detailed description of them. I was just around the corner when the highway guys called saying they had been spotted and that the three offenders were out of the house and running. They managed to catch one of them at the front gate but the other two were on the toe and heading in my direction.

I saw these two come flying around the corner on the footpath and into my street. I slammed on the brakes and called out the window, 'You two stop or I'll send the dog.' They slowed to a jog, looked straight at

144

me then decided to go for it. They both put their heads back, pumped their legs as fast as they could go and sprinted. One of them turned left and ran into a block of units disappearing from sight. The other ran across the road and, in doing so, put himself into Merlin's line of sight. He had been watching both from the rear of the car and knew something was on due to the lights and sirens and fast driving in our car. I popped the rear tailgate and yelled out to the runner who was by now about 100m in front of us. He was a further 100m from the main street. If he makes it there then there is no way I'm going to be able to catch him and I cannot track or search the area with all those other people walking around. I'm not the fastest runner in the world and there is no way I would be able to run him down in time. As there were no other police in the vicinity able to help, I had no option.

'Police, stop or I'll send the dog.'

The thief looked over his shoulder and kept running. He knew he wasn't far off making his escape; only a few more metres and he was home free.

I gave Merlin a command, released him and watched my own personal black-and-tan crook-seeking missile take off after its target. He pulled his ears back and began to easily run down the hapless runner. As he got closer I saw the runner look back but keep running, I also heard him cry out in panic as he realised that only about 5m from the main road Merlin was on him. Merlin jumped on the runner's back taking him down in a beautiful from-behind tackle that any rugby player would be proud of. He clamped his jaws down on his shoulder as they hit the hard and very hot concrete footpath. I arrived just as this very desperate man started to slap Merlin about his head. All this did was make him angry and in turn he increased the pressure on his bite. The more you fight him the harder he fights you.

I pushed this guy back onto the ground as he tried to get up with

Merlin still attached to his shoulder! I'll give this guy credit for being tough enough to keep trying. However, he was fighting a losing battle with a police dog team that was not going to let him go. I gave Merlin a command and he let go with his grip, returning to my side but never for one second taking his eyes off his quarry. I gave him a genuine and proud 'good boy' for his excellent arrest. Quite unbelievably, the runner wasn't finished; he was desperate to get away. He jumped up while I was getting back up via the police radio as well as an ambulance for him. I reached forward and tried to grab his arm. This action of course bought Merlin back into the action. He jumped forward and took hold of the crook's lower leg. The man cried out then turned and planted a roundhouse punch to the side of my head. As I have said before, I have a huge, thick head so there was no real damage done but I'm not a punching bag and I won't back down either. In self defence, I struck his chin which sent him to the ground with Merlin still holding his shin. I yelled, 'Just give up mate, this is ridiculous, you can't win.'

Just then, a couple of other police cars arrived. I picked up Merlin's lead and gave him a command. He let go and again returned to my side. The other police took over and started to handcuff him. Can you believe it, he started to fight with them throwing punches and kicking and screaming until eventually he was handcuffed and put in a police truck, taken to hospital with some cuts and bruises then charged with all the associated offences. One of the police who went with him to hospital asked him why he had fought us so hard. His reply was that he had never been in trouble before and didn't want to go to gaol because his father would kill him! I think his father is now the least of his problems.

Off Duty

When we're off duty the work doesn't really stop. Just because it's not a work day doesn't mean I lock Merlin in his kennel and forget about him until it's time to go to work again. On days off, I spend at least an hour of the day exercising and training with him. The Dog Squad is not a job, it is a lifestyle. If you want to get the best out of your dog then you have to put in the time and that means your own time as well.

Usually I take him for a long walk of between 5 and 10km, depending on the weather and my mood. I have a friend who runs a local takeaway shop about 5km from where I live. Usually we would walk there on a Sunday morning. My friend Tony would always have sausages and other fast food heating under the front counter of his shop. One Sunday morning as we were passing, Tony's young son was behind the counter. He saw us coming and raced out the front carrying a huge beef sausage from the shop.

He ran up to Merlin and dropped it at his feet. Now, Merlin being a good police dog looked back at me and sat down. He knew that if he went to pick it up he was going to be in trouble. (We discourage our dogs from taking food as there are people out there who would gladly bait them.) I just looked at the pathetic begging expression he had put on and gave in. I gave him his word to eat and I don't think

147

the sausage even touched the sides as it disappeared down his happy little throat. Now we had set a precedent. Every single time we passed Tony's shop, without fail Merlin would sit down and wait to be served a sausage. He had a new best friend in Tony's son and I was unable to keep walking until Garbage Guts had been fed.

The one good thing about having a police dog at home is the security. Nobody, but nobody would make it more than a few steps into my yard before they were confronted by the four-legged alarm system. Merlin, however, would sometimes pull swifties on the unsuspecting. The place I used to live in was a single-storey wooden house set about 1m above the ground on stilts. This was a great place for Merlin to relax on very hot summer days. In the rear yard I had a granny flat which at the time was rented to a friend. She had organised to have a rental company deliver her a fridge. I agreed to wait at home and let the guy in. When he turned up I pointed him towards a side gate which led down a path to the granny flat. I had just watched him push the fridge through on his trolley when I remembered Merlin was out and relaxing under the house. Uh oh.

I raced to the side window just as the delivery guy passed by, oblivious to the two beady orange eyes following his every move. I saw Merlin emerge from under the house and slink up behind the delivery bloke not making a single sound. I yelled out 'No!'. I ran from inside the house onto the back balcony around the granny flat and up onto the side path. When I got to where the rental guy was, I breathed a sigh of relief. He was standing on top of the fridge trying to climb into a neighbour's overhanging tree branch. Merlin was seated in front of the fridge growling. He had let this guy pass into his yard to trap him. He was being a sneak because most other dogs would have run straight up to the fence and barked at the stranger, warning them not to come in. Not Merlin. He let them in, then bailed them up, God love him. I apologised, gave the delivery guy a Coke and a smile, then let him get on with his day.

There is one thing about dogs and all of them have it—they are pack animals and will always act as such when given the opportunity. Merlin is no different. He is a pack dog with one slight difference from the vast majority; he is a pack dog with a huge ambition. He wants to be the boss but if he wants to be the boss he has to beat the boss and that's me. Every year, about June, we would have it out. Usually we would be out on our local oval. I would be throwing a baseball for him to chase as his sprint training. He would run out, fetch the ball and bring it back. I would give him a command and he would give me the ball.

This time he fetched the ball and came back. I gave him the command and he just stared at me. I gave it again and put my hand on the ball. Now he was growling and biting down harder on the ball. He also started to pull back his ears. Okay, here we go again I thought. I had to pick him up and put him on his back. This is a submissive position for a dog and not an easy thing to do when the dog does not want to be put there. The dog slobber started to fly as he spat out the ball and held my arm at the elbow in his mouth. He wasn't biting hard but he was letting me know his intentions. I ended up on top holding his neck and staring directly into his eyes, not blinking and not looking away. He was staring straight back in defiance. After about twenty seconds he looked away. I had won and was still the leader of the pack. I took the ball and threw it. He ran out, picked it up and returned. I gave him a command and he let go of the ball, just as if nothing had ever happened at all. The last thing I want to do is hurt Merlin in any way. I had to be very firm and strong with him in this instance. I was concentrating on eye contact to defeat him. If he had won, then I may as well have packed up and left the Dog Squad. If he thinks that he's better than me then he will never respect me or do anything I ask of him. If I'm still in charge then he will go anywhere and do anything I ask him. That's how it works. If you think that you're going to come up to Merlin or any police dogs and try to stare them down, then watch out. This is a direct challenge to them and they will react. Remember that there is no bluff with a police dog.

High or Low —The Nose Knows

These two jobs occurred in the same area but at different times of the day. They demonstrate how good the sense of smell of a police dog is, how they can pick who is sweating bullets and who is just plain sweating. The suburb is Kirribilli is nestled under the Sydney Harbour Bridge and has some of the most beautiful views of Sydney Harbour. There are both free-standing houses and multi-storey unit blocks with a number of office buildings thrown in as well. Crooks love to come here to steal from some of the more upmarket residences in Sydney.

This fine spring morning was no different. I was just trawling around trying to see if I could spot anybody who didn't fit in and enjoying the view of the harbour.

Some of the local boys had been called to a man who was acting suspiciously near the fire exit of one of the multi-storey unit blocks. Just as they arrived, they saw this bloke coming out of the fire escape holding a plasma screen TV. He saw them, dropped the TV and legged it. One of the police officers jumped out of the patrol car and took off after him calling over the police radio that he was, 'in foot pursuit of a Break and Enter offender heading east through the park under the

151

bridge.' Meanwhile his mate was driving around in an effort to cut the runner off. I was getting excited at the prospect of such a juicy job dishing itself up on a boring weekday morning. I switched on all my bells and whistles and headed over as fast as I could—I was only a kilometre away. Probably ten seconds later, the officer in foot pursuit and puffing very heavily called that he had lost sight of the runner in a block of units. He knew I was coming and waited where he was.

When I arrived and saw the number of people walking around I knew that it would be pointless for Merlin to try and track. We were going to have to do this by walking on lead and hoping he could pick this guy up on the wind. As the chasing police officer had lost sight of this guy very quickly, I was pretty sure he had gone to ground hoping not to be found.

I got an excited Merlin out of the car and started to walk in the direction the crook had last run. When I came around the side of the building he had run into I was a bit dismayed to find there were four options of escape open to him. Two down alleys and two along a small dead-end street which ran up into a local private school. We started along the street to see if he had gone under a car or was hiding in someone's front yard. Merlin did manage to locate two young ladies enjoying a coffee on their front balcony but I could tell that he wasn't really interested. They were definitely not giving off the vibe we were after. They did, however help me out a great deal by letting me know that they had been there for half an hour and nobody had run out into the street.

We turned around and went straight into one of the alleys that snaked through a couple of units coming out at the second alley's entrance. I was starting to smell blood in the water. I knew this crook had to be in here somewhere. Merlin picked up on my mood, dragging me in for the kill. We came into the courtyard of a unit block which had probably been around since the forties. There was a staircase leading up to a balcony which gave access to the rear of all the units and on ground level everyone's private lock-up laundries. As we passed the second last laundry Merlin stopped, snapped his head around and dragged me to the door. He started to wag his tail and growl at the door, eventually barking which told me someone was behind it. I tried the door but found that it was well and truly locked on the outside with a padlock. The door however did not go all the way to the roof; there was a gap of about half a metre. I banged on the door and yelled out, 'It's the police, come out now, I know you're in there, mate.' Nothing.

I did the same again with Merlin getting more and more worked up. He started to block his front paws on the door in an effort to get in. Still nothing. I managed to get up and peer inside the laundry. It was pitch dark and appeared to be full of debris and rubbish. I used my torch but I could not see anything resembling a human being. Merlin was insistent. I looked at him and said, 'Mate, you had better be right or I'm going to look bloody stupid.'

I got onto the police radio and called in the other police. There were quite a few more by now including the shift-supervising sergeant. I left Merlin sitting at the door just in case the crook decided to leave and walked out to inform the locals of what had happened. I told them we were probably going to have to force the door as this guy wouldn't come out. The sergeant looked at me and asked if I was sure. I took the plunge and said, 'Yep, one hundred per cent he is in there.' He told me he trusted me and that the Police Department would fix any damaged caused to the door.

By now I was praying Merlin was right.

We returned to the laundry to find Merlin still sitting and staring at the door. I put him on lead and watched with baited breath as the local boys forced in the door and started to rip out the rubbish. Merlin was back to going crazy and straining at his leash when, after about the fourth piece of rubbish, a body was dragged out from the dark. Bingo, it was the runner! The sergeant turned and looked at me and all he could say was, 'Unbelievable'. I gave Merlin a big pat on his flank told him he was a good boy then turned to the other boys and said, 'Never in doubt boys, never in doubt.'

The next powerful nose story comes from the same area with the local police chasing another Break and Enter offender from a private house not far from where we had caught the first runner. He had been spotted coming out a side window with a laptop computer under his arm. He was with his girlfriend who was playing cockatoo for him. She spotted the police and sounded out the warning. One of them chased down the girlfriend and the second officer tailed the Break and Enter merchant into a school before losing sight of him. I was called in just after midnight. As we were only about ten minutes behind, the track was still 'hot' and Merlin was snorting up the pavement tracking with great focus and drive. We steamed through the centre of the school and out into a rear playground, locating the stolen laptop under a seat as we went. The playground had an exit out to the street. I thought 'Bugger, he's probably continued on through'. We were just about at the exit when Merlin made a fast right-hand turn and began circling a huge Moreton Bay Fig tree. His tail was up and he was growling. I put the torch on the tree but could not see a thing. Merlin started to bark, indicating that someone was up there. I left him sitting at the base and walked out about 50m. Using my torch I scanned the upper branches. There he was about 15–20m up the tree. I shouted, 'Come on down, mate, the game's up.' He refused to move until I took Merlin away. Not wanting to climb the tree myself I put him on lead and watched as the crook came down and was arrested. The love birds had come all the way from Penrith in Sydney's far west to, as they put it 'Do a little thieving.'

Well, he ended up doing a little 'time' for his trouble.

The last one is a beauty. We were over in Redfern looking for a stolen car that had been seen in the area and chased a few times by the police. I heard a call come over the police radio for a dog to go to Channel D, which covers the Lower North Shore up to the Northern Beaches area. I changed over and immediately heard an officer calling a foot pursuit. I immediately got a little shot of excitement as these are usually great dog jobs. I got even more interested when it was revealed that he was chasing an armed robber who had just held up the Neutral Bay post office. This was the same armed robber who had been terrorising the lower North Shore for about two months, committing between twenty and thirty armed hold ups. The pursuing officer was driving by on his own and had just been lucky enough to glance over to see the crook walk casually out of the front doors with a balaclava on. He pulled it off and strolled off down the main road as if nothing had happened. This guy had been able to evade police on every occasion but had slipped up this time. Police were desperate to capture him and take him off the street. I called on to the job over the police radio and high tailed it over to Neutral Bay. About half way across the Harbour Bridge, the pursuing officer had lost sight of the armed robber who had disappeared into a residential block of houses. This type of job had attracted a lot of police and a large perimeter was set up quite quickly. I knew it was going to be hard to get a result as there were a lot of people out and about and there were going to be people in and around their houses. I pulled up next to the police officer who had been chasing him and got an excited Merlin out for the hunt. The officer pointed to the front yard of a house and told me that the crook came around the corner and disappeared somewhere in the yard. I started to feel a bit more confident as Merlin started to drag me in to the yard and put his nose to the ground telling me that someone had just been through there. I harnessed him into his tracking gear and away we went.

We powered down the side of the house then through a hole in the wood panel fence. Merlin didn't miss a beat as he continued on almost ripping out my arms as my large carcass got held up in the hole. We tracked over the next three yards jumping the fences as we went. Even though it was the middle of the day in summer and very hot, Merlin's pace did not falter and I thought we must be getting close. We came to the last yard which was overgrown with waist-high bushes and vines. Merlin pulled straight into the seemingly impenetrable mass of vegetation.

I held him up and shouted out, 'Police, come out or I'll send in the dog.' Merlin was barking and growling leaving no one in doubt that he meant business. I was convinced that this robber was in there. I yelled out again, and again I heard no response. I gave Merlin a command and released him into the bush, losing sight of him almost immediately. I heard him fight his way through the bushes, all the time using his nose to try and locate his target. Eventually Merlin emerged beside the house, having come out of the jungle and under the floor area holding something black in his mouth. I called him over to find he was carrying a black balaclava. Damn, I thought, the crook's still running. If he were in here, Merlin would have found him and brought the rest with him, not just his disguise. I told him he was a good boy and took possession of the evidence, taking care not to contaminate it any further so we could get a DNA sample from it. I thought that it was going to be a very difficult proposition to get a result as the crook was by now out of the police perimeter and mingling with the public. All we had to go on was a Pacific Islander male, large build with short hair wearing blue denim shorts, black t-shirt and white runners carrying a black bag with about five thousand dollars inside.

I couldn't track as there were police all along the front of the houses and members of the public having a look to see what was going on. On the other side of the street was a row of unit blocks which had a very large commercial car park for the shops at the top end. Not good odds for us having a success. Even so, it's not over till it's over so I put a now-panting Merlin into his lead and we went for a walk. We started at a block of units opposite the last house we had searched, carefully checking the car park and bin areas. Merlin was at this stage very disinterested and in dire need of a drink and rest. As we came to the top of the unit car park near the commercial car park, this changed in an instant.

Between these two areas is a small electrical transformer station which has a set of stairs leading up to a small balcony behind a garden-style wall. Merlin's tail went straight up with his hackles. He pumped out his chest and lifted his nose, barking out to me that someone was hiding up behind that wall. We sprinted up the stairs and saw our armed robber lying flat behind the brick wall on the balcony. He didn't even look up. He was probably hoping that this was a dream and that he wasn't about to have all those armed robberies come crashing down around his ears. Sorry mate, this is the real deal and you're in it up to your neck. Merlin was panting and growling at him as he was led away by the local detectives who were very happy that this serial armed robber was finally where he belonged, in custody. He had picked this guy out of all the scents he would have been picking up in the area.

The crook could see the writing on the wall and took the detectives back to the car park where he had hidden his takings from the robbery. He threw his hands up to most of the armed robberies that had been committed and is now serving a lengthy prison sentence. Usually the best results come when we least expect it. These incidents just highlight how powerful and discerning a police dog's nose can be. It still amazes me every time he locates someone with it.

Low Act

As police, we have to act impartially and not take things personally. In this story it was very hard to control the emotions when I saw what was happening to my mate. It was mid-summer about three in the morning and I was starting to think about going home. A call came over the police radio concerning the victim of an armed robbery who had followed the five perpetrators to a park in North Ryde. As luck would have it we were only a few minutes from the very same park. I sparked up a little and turned to Merlin, 'Come on, mate, one more little job and we can go home.'

As we were nearby, I drove up to a point near the park with my lights off; no need to let them know I was coming. I listened intently to the police radio who told me there were five bad guys. One of them had used a large knife to rob the victim and one of them had told the victim he had a gun but had not pulled it out and shown him. Both were drunk and wearing white singlets and white baseball caps. To make it easier, the police radio was in direct contact with the victim of the robbery via his mobile phone. He was hiding in bushes at the edge of the park, keeping an eye on his attackers.

I stopped about 200m from the park edge and waited while the local police set a nice quiet perimeter around the park. I was going in with four other police officers and Merlin. We all put on our ballistic vests (ballistic vests for dogs had not yet been introduced); these are full Kevlar with a ceramic chest plate, just in case there really was a gun. It would make it hard for us to move quickly but better if we started to receive any gunfire. It was pitch black in the park but we could hear the crooks inside laughing and shouting with each other. One in particular was big mouthing about how funny it looked when they 'rolled' the guy and held the knife at his throat. I thought how funny is it going to look when you realise you're surrounded and realise how much trouble you are in.

Merlin was starting to growl and pull hard towards the noisy group of drunks. I held him up and patted his flank, whispering, 'Quiet mate, quiet.' He settled down but was fully focused on the noise in front. Soon after, the trap was set and we moved in close. We managed to get in to about 5m of the group who were still big noting their criminal exploits when Merlin couldn't control himself anymore and let fly with his opinion of their behaviour. His barking made everybody jump, especially the crooks who looked in our direction with bug eyes when I lit them up with my torch and yelled, 'Police, get on the ground.'

Two of them complied immediately but three of them ran, including two with white singlets and white caps on. They headed straight towards a tree line and creek which was situated at the edge of the park with a line of houses running along the other side. There were two cops standing between them and the creek. The officers with me were busy arresting the first two who had given up. I started off after them but wasn't going to catch them with all the equipment I was wearing. I saw the two perimeter police tackle the third runner but the two singlet wearers, who were still armed as far as I was concerned, kept on sprinting for the creek line. I had them lit up with my torch and knew Merlin had them targeted.

I yelled, 'Police, stop running or I'll send the dog.' They kept on going not even looking back over their shoulders. Just as I was about to let Merlin off his lead two other police officers came barrelling out of the dark getting in between the runners and us. I yelled out, 'All police stop running, the dog is coming.' Luckily both officers heard me and had the sense to listen. Both stopped and stood there like statues. Just as they did so the two runners disappeared from sight into thick scrub which led straight into the creek. I gave Merlin a command and released him from his lead. He was so wound up he literally exploded out of the starting gate, pulling back his ears as he powered away. He ran straight past the two police statues and disappeared into the same scrub. I was doing my best to keep up but by the time I made it there I could neither hear nor see anything. I was joined by the now reanimated officers who followed in behind.

About ten seconds later I heard Merlin's, 'I've found someone' bark. It was probably 50m from where we were standing. I picked up the pace running through the knee-deep creek and onto a grass embankment. I noticed that the barking had stopped and a panicky type of squeal had taken over. As I came up over the embankment, I saw Merlin holding one of the white singlet-wearing criminals by his left leg. He was squealing and trying to break free by kicking out. The thing that really increased my heart rate was the second crook that ran up behind Merlin and gave him a full kick from behind to his ribs, not once but twice. I could see Merlin was trying to look back to see who was kicking him but would not let go of the crook he already had. I was by now at full running pace as the low thug wound up to kick again. Just as he was coming forward I came in from his side and pushed him away on his left shoulder. Because I was running at full speed, my hand bounced off his shoulder and struck him squarely on his cheek. This caused quite a large wound and pushed him about 2m onto the ground from Merlin who was able to turn his attention back to the first crook. I was fuming that he had been king hit like that but was happy he had been strong enough to hold his ground with the first crook. I gave him a command and he let go of the first guy who was still crying and whining, certainly not full of the bravado and hot wind from a few minutes ago. He was taken away by other police who had arrived. They told me that the knife had been found on the ground just where the foot pursuit had started.

I turned and saw the kicking hero with two other officers who had called an ambulance as he was bleeding quite heavily from the hole in his cheek. I wanted to vent my opinion straight at him but took a deep breath and walked away which was probably the best thing to do. I got Merlin back to the car and touched his left rib cage. I could feel him move away and give me a little growl. He was tender but not too bad. I took him to the vet the next day where he was cleared of any broken bones. Thankfully he only had bruising. Even so, I still get a little cranky when I think about Merlin taking those cheap shots, but I have to accept this as part of the job.

About a year later we went to court over this matter where the kicker was cleared because it was my word against his and, anyway, his mother gave evidence that her son was scared of dogs and could not possibly have gone close enough to kick any dog because he was so scared.

Afterwards I was leaving the court house when the crook followed me out into the car park being careful not to get too far away from his support crew. He sneered at me and wished me better luck next time. Normally I'd just laugh and walk away as it's water off a duck's back. Right or wrong, I turned back to him noticing the large scar on his cheek and smiled. I just said, 'Mate, every day for the rest of your life when you look in the mirror you're going to have a little reminder of me and my dog, see ya.'

He had no come-back except to stand there with a dumb look on his face. I just walked away.

Will You Take the Curtain or the Door?

It was just before Christmas and we were on an afternoon shift about 8pm. This time of the year, everybody's running around like headless chooks getting ready for the big day and attending Christmas functions so there is generally a lot of cash being held by pubs and clubs. This brings out a dangerous kind of predator, the armed robber. They consist of two basic types: first is the professional who checks out his target properly and strikes when the odds are stacked in his favour. These guys are in and out very quickly and do not want to get caught up in anything except getting their cash. Most of these crooks will get away with it many times until they are eventually caught or are given up by another crook. (There is no such thing as honour among thieves.)

The second is the opportunist or amateur who believes there is easy money to be had if you have the guts to do it. They don't do much research and generally it is their first time. Some guys paint themselves into a corner and can see no other way out other than trying to steal the money. A good example is a guy who was in charge of his church's money, about twenty thousand dollars. He took it and punted it all in a day at the horse races. The next day he hid in the roof of a bank near Redfern Police Station and ambushed the manager as he came in. Other employees had seen him and ran up to the station. In about two minutes police had surrounded the bank and this guy was arrested trying to run out the back. Here is a guy who was a committed Christian and had never been in trouble with the police for anything except now for armed robbery at his first desperate attempt.

This story starts with an armed hold up alarm coming from a pub on Burwood Road at Burwood in Sydney's south-west. I was about five minutes away and listened as a local crew who just happened to be passing called off there. About twenty seconds later I heard a call over the police radio, 'Burwood 15 urgent, the armed robbers are still here on the first floor and they're armed with pistols.' I put my foot to the floor as I activated my lights and sirens and arrived about two minutes later.

As I pulled up I saw the local police supervisor who was wearing his ballistic vest and a worried expression. He asked whether I would go up and see if they were still there. The original responding police had withdrawn down the stairs and formed the best perimeter they could. Just as I was about to answer, a mate of mine Paul, who is also in the Dog Squad, turned up and said 'let's go in'. I spoke to the original police who told me that when they had gone up to the gaming room, two very large males wearing blue overalls and balaclavas had pointed handguns at them but not fired. They believed that the two of them were still up there. I put on my vest and was joined by Paul who was going to cover me as I went up the stairs with Merlin. As we got closer to the top I was sweating and had a very dry throat; I could feel my heart beating and the adrenalin starting to flow. This was neither a movie nor a video game. At the time I thought I was going to have to confront armed offenders who may try to kill me. Anybody who says that that prospect does not make them nervous or apprehensive is either a liar or mad.

As we reached the top step, I kept as low as possible with Merlin on my left side. I drew my pistol and started to scan the room. All I could see were poker machines in the centre and along the wall of the room which was about 20x5m. At the front of the room was a large window covered by a thin white curtain. Behind that curtain I could see a human figure standing up. I told Paul that I thought someone was behind it and that he should cover in the opposite direction when I went in. He nodded and I started into the room bent over and pointing my pistol at the figure. About 3m from the window, Merlin started to growl at the figure which had still not moved. I yelled, 'Police, you behind the curtain come out with your hands up, now.' The figure did not move. I yelled the same thing again which started Merlin barking and fighting to get behind the curtain. I wasn't prepared to take any chances so I kept Merlin on his lead and, after putting my pistol back into its holster, I gave the figure an almighty shove with my right hand. As soon as I did this I realised how bloody stupid I was. I had just slammed my hand into a concrete statue which bounced into the window frame and back onto me. I can tell you I swore as I was in a very bad position for no good reason other than I was a dill. Merlin had come around and sniffed at the statue, losing interest just about immediately. I looked down at him and said, 'What a pair of bloody idiots we are.'

I had to forget it as there was still the little problem of the two armed robbers. I put aside the pain in my right hand and continued to search. Paul had seen the whole thing and just shook his head when he looked at us. As we moved along the opposite side of the wall to the stairs, Merlin indicated a black carry bag which was sitting on a stool next to a closed door. As far as I was concerned, the room was now clear. I looked into the bag and to my surprise I saw a .45 calibre handgun, balaclava, cash and a man's wallet. The bloody idiots had left the money behind. I pushed on the door and found that it opened. Entering very warily I saw that it was the manager's office containing the closed safe and empty cash trays for the poker machines. I also saw that the window onto the roof was open. I checked the drop then sent Merlin through, following him up very quickly. The roof area was wide and flat leading onto other adjacent roofs along the line of shops. I thought we might still be half a chance.

Merlin started to drag me towards the next roof so I held on and followed. We covered three more roofs then jumped down onto an awning then into a car park where the scent stopped. They had managed to get away in the car they had waiting there. There were just two things that had gone wrong for them. First, the bag we found belonged to the armed robbers and had the owner's wallet containing all his identification inside it. (He was seen carrying it into the room on surveillance cameras) and second, they had used their own car for the getaway. Again this was captured on surveillance video at the rear of the business at which it was parked. They were both local men and were arrested by detectives and other police a few hours later. It had been their first attempt at armed robbery and most likely their last.

Curiosity Killed the Crook

It was one of those nights when I wished I was back home in bed. It was mid-winter and it had been raining non-stop for about a week. I was just counting down the hours as we had been driving around aimlessly for the past six, with not a single job anywhere. As is often the case in police work, just as you're about to give up on anything happening, it happens. I heard a call from a police motorcyclist who had almost been hit by a car on Parramatta Road, Leichhardt, an inner city suburb. He had turned and started after the car which, it turned out, was a stolen Subaru WRX. These things are hard enough to catch in the dry let alone the wet with their four-wheel-drive turbo engines. Luckily though, just as he was about to self-terminate the pursuit, the crook did it for him. In a wave of spray and sliding tyres he had lost control and slammed the car head on into a brick wall, showering the glass and car parts in all directions. Of course he was completely unscathed and took off like a rabbit. All the cyclist saw was a yellow t-shirt disappearing into the safety of the dark. I was there in a matter of minutes glad for the opportunity to work, even if it was pissing down rain.

I collected Merlin who had a very big yawn and stretch as he emerged out of his warm dry car and into the bracing weather. It was raining but not hard enough to affect our track. I harnessed him up took him to the driver's side of the stolen car and gave him his command. Merlin started to search for the scent and within a few seconds he had found what he wanted and we were tracking the driver along the footpath. We kept on going all the way down to the City West Link expressway. This is a major road linking the city of Sydney to Parramatta Road. Because it was 4am, there was absolutely no one around and hardly any vehicles using the link. The rain was steady but not affecting Merlin or his incredible nose. A few times along the track he would put his nose too close to the ground and snort up water from a puddle which made him cough and splutter but never lose concentration. We turned west and powered on through the weather finally coming up to Balmain Road where we changed direction again heading south back towards the centre of Leichhardt.

It wasn't long and we turned left back into the same street that the WRX had crashed in. I looked down and could still see a plume of smoke and steam coming from the wreckage. By this time the fire brigade had turned up and was assessing the damage. We kept on going and I noticed that Merlin was pulling just that little bit harder and starting to lift his head and look around a bit more. Then about 100m up in front I saw a figure emerge from a yard on the left of the road and look down at the scene of the crash. There was just enough light to make out that he was wearing a yellow t-shirt.

I crouched down and began to move towards him. Merlin had also seen him and was skull dragging me in his direction. The figure moved back into the yard disappearing from my sight. I wasn't worried as I knew Merlin's nose would get us there with more accuracy than a cruise missile. In we came, closer and closer, 20 then 10m until I saw him come out again and look at the crash. Incredibly he still had not seen or heard us approach. I pulled Merlin in close to my side and about a metre from behind the runner I yelled, 'Police, get on the ground.' This set off Merlin who barked his head off assisting me with the desired effect of making the crook jump ten feet into the air with a terrified look stamped on his face. He didn't talk at first then started to tell lies in an attempt to convince me of his innocence,

'It wasn't me, I'm too young to drive.'

'I live here but I lost my key.'

'You can't prove it was me, no one saw me there.'

'I was on my way home and I wanted to stay out of the rain.'

None of these utterings made any sense and he lived in Strathfield which is about 20km from where we were. Eventually he was able to face up to what he had done and confessed to being the driver. I asked him why he had done the big loop and was watching the crash. He told me he just wanted to see if the car was on fire and wanted to see the fire brigade put it out. I shook my head and marched him back to the scene where he was promptly arrested by the cyclist and put in the back of a police truck. Obviously not just a car thief but a pyromaniac as well.

Colour Blind

There are a great many police officers out there who have learned the hard way that police dogs do not recognise police uniforms or see the colour blue. If in a confrontational situation the police dog will usually take on the closest person they believe is a threat to themselves or their handler. Merlin is no different and has taught this lesson on a number of occasions. There are two which really stick out.

The first lesson was given to a female probationary constable in Cabramatta. We had been called to a Break and Enter at a house on one of the main roads about ten in the morning. The local police had done all the right things and had the house surrounded on all sides. I was in the area trawling around and was able to get to the scene in about two minutes.

Just as I was jumping the side fence to access the rear patio, I saw movement inside the house. Merlin saw it too with his ears pricking up and tail starting to wag—he knew that it was game on. A neighbour told me that the people who lived there were overseas and there definitely should not be anybody in there. We ran to the rear and saw broken glass from a kitchen window strewn over the patio. The window was about 180cm from the ground. It was then I saw our crook running back and forth in a mad panic inside the house. He was looking for a way out but there most definitely was none. I yelled out, 'Mate, it's the police, come out or I'm sending the dog in, I can see you and there's no escape.' About five seconds later the crook walked dejectedly into the kitchen and gave up. I told him to come out the window but he refused. He didn't want to come out unless I took the dog away. By this time Merlin was barking and salivating on the end of his lead. I just told him that if he did as he was told then he would not get hurt. He still didn't believe me but stuck his head out of the window just far enough for me to grab a hold of his collar with my free hand. I got a good grip and yanked him with all the might I could muster. Surprisingly, he came flying out of the window and over my head with ease and crashed into an outdoor furniture setting on the patio. I had a good hold of Merlin who followed his flight and lunged at him. At this exact same moment a very young and enthusiastic probationary constable came out of left field and jumped on top of the crook in an attempt to handcuff him. Unfortunately for her this put her backside between the crook and Merlin who was quite excited by now and took his opportunity as it presented itself. He just got one of his upper K9's into this soft fleshy skin and opened it up. She yelped and jumped out of the way which only opened the flesh up further. She was rubbing the wound which was bleeding quite freely and giving us a very dirty look at the same time. She spat out the words, 'Doesn't he know I'm a copper too?'

'Sorry, but no,' I said. 'You shouldn't get between a police dog and crooks, it hurts.' Other wiser police had been watching and took a wide berth around Merlin before handcuffing the Break and Enter merchant. They were all smiling and telling the young bleeding cop, 'We told you to wait.' She went to hospital and had five stitches to close up her wound. The crook was taken away and spent about a year in gaol for his bungled Break and Enters.

The second 'friendly fire' incident occurred in the middle of the

Sydney Central Business District during a protest. We had been called in to assist the local and patrol support group police with a protest of some kind. (I've been to so many I don't bother to worry about why they're there anymore.) Things were going smoothly with the crowd moving along blowing horns, whistles and banging drums in tune with their chants. This was until they reached the front of Central Railway Station on Broadway when they all sat down and blocked this major intersection. The police started the laborious job of moving the protestors one by one and putting them in the rear of trucks. There was a lot of screaming and flailing of arms and legs but the police were soon getting on top while the Dog Squad watched their backs. Merlin was barking and carrying on each time one of the protestors was dragged by.

All of a sudden I got a tap on my right shoulder. I was just starting to say the word 'no' when Merlin spun around like a snake and bit down on to the arm of a chief inspector in full uniform. I yelled out a command as quickly as possible and he let go. I got one of the most incredulous looks I have ever had from a commissioned officer. He was holding his arm and staring at us in complete shock and horror. To rub salt into the wound Merlin came at him a second time which made him stumble back in double-quick time. Unlike the probationer, this officer has been around long enough to know better. He should have called out to me then told me he was going to come in closer. He only got a few lacerations and some bruising on his arm along with a battered ego. I spoke to him afterwards and he couldn't understand why Merlin had bitten him! I couldn't understand why he still couldn't work it out for himself. Police dogs don't care who you are or how high a rank you have, if you come too close they don't like it and they take action. There is no bluff with a police dog.

Watch Your Step

One of the things I hate about summer is the mix of alcohol and hot weather. These two combine to turn usually normal mild-mannered people into objectionable monsters. It was about a week before Christmas which is when most business Christmas parties are in full swing. We had been called to the car park behind a pub in Berowra which is in the very north of suburban Sydney. There had been a punch up there between work colleagues who had then turned on the first police to arrive—they had joined forces and were now fighting them! We arrived to a scene of mayhem and violence. There were four police officers fighting about a dozen drunks. That's not fair, so I decided to even things up. I released Merlin from the back of the car and charged straight in to the fight. I yelled out 'Police, get back.' The rest was pretty self explanatory even to a drunk. Merlin was driving his rear legs and spraying saliva every time he barked and growled.

Just about all the drunks took the hint and dispersed, all except two. These two drunken clowns wanted to keep on going. One of them was quickly subdued and slammed into the ground by the exhausted police. He fought and spat until the very end when he was thrown into the back of a police truck.

The second guy was a big one and was putting up a real fight. He had knocked one of the police down with a punch to the face that had

174

split his now bleeding lip. He turned to the second cop who had no option but to strike him to the leg with a police baton. I was about 50m from this incident as it happened. I turned Merlin's focus away from the first fighter who was by now in the truck and mouthing off about how he was going to kill us and our families. We sprinted over just in time to see the big drunk shove the baton-swinging officer in the chest. I yelled out, 'Police get on the ground'. The drunk took one look at Merlin and took off running. I yelled again, 'Police, stop or I'm going to release the dog.' Merlin was by now outpacing me and I had him by the very end of his lead. The drunk vaulted a fence and disappeared into the dark. I was never going to catch him this way and there were no other police around to help so I yelled out a command and let Merlin off his lead.

He cleared the same fence by 2m on either side and a good metre and a half over the top. Not missing a beat, he speared off into the dark hot on the trail of the drunk while I lumbered behind in a vain attempt to keep sight of them but failed miserably. (You try running fast in boots, overalls, soft body armour and a belt weighed down by handcuffs, radio, gun, spare ammo and other bits and pieces.) Thankfully it didn't take long for Merlin to catch up with his prey. I had seen him with my torch running at full pace about 30m in front when he came to a skidding halt and darted off into the yard of a house and disappeared. A very short time later I heard a crashing sound then Merlin barking followed by a man calling desperately for help. I wasn't sure about exactly what had happened but I was sure that Merlin was on top of the situation. I chugged into the yard but couldn't see anything except a balcony down the side of the house and a steep drop off beside it. I could still hear the male calling for help and Merlin growling. I could also hear the sound of fabric tearing. I walked along the balcony to the end and looked down over the edge noticing that there was no rail.

I laughed out loud when I saw the drunk wedged between the house wall, supporting beam of the balcony and a hot water system which left him about 70cm-square of room. He could not move. To make it worse, Merlin had managed to push his snout in far enough to grab hold of his jeans and was trying to drag his whole body through a 10–15cm hole.

I called Merlin off and he returned back to my side on the balcony. The drunk was crying now and told me how he had run onto the balcony and seen Merlin bearing down on him about half way across. He had panicked and started to run not bothering to watch where he was running to. He had gone straight off the end of the balcony and wedged himself into his current position. He complained that he had re-broken his foot which was killing him with pain even in his intoxicated state. He told me that Merlin had come to the edge of the balcony and stopped, obviously not drunk or silly enough to go over the edge. He had run back around and started to bark and pull at his jeans. We had to get rescue there to pull him out, then take him to hospital. The ridiculous thing was that neither of the drunks had ever been in trouble with the police. Both just managed to scramble their brains enough with alcohol and heat to turn themselves into lunatics.

Russians in Chatswood

This is a bizarre story which begins with me sitting at traffic lights on the Pacific Highway at Chatswood. It was about 11pm on a Saturday night with all the usual weekend mayhem going on. I just happened to look up at a high-rise unit block. In doing so, I saw something you don't see every day. There was a body being held upside down over a balcony on about the twentieth floor. There were two people holding the body while a third appeared to be hitting it with a length of wood. I blinked and looked up again. Yep, that is what I saw. I got out and looked up, hearing screaming from both men and women. There were pot plants and furniture being thrown around and over the edge of the same balcony. The body had been pulled back over and a general fight appeared to be going on. Just as I was about to call the job over the police radio I was spared the effort.

'North Shore cars or any car in the vicinity, Brown Street, Chatswood there is a fight going on inside the unit with knives involved. There is also a report of items being thrown over the balcony on to the street below.'

I jumped straight on telling them what I had seen. I went to the main entrance of the high-rise to wait for back up. Merlin sat patiently by my side unaware of what was going on twenty floors up. Just before other police arrived, the fire escape opened up and a man about twenty-five years old emerged holding his right arm. I also happened to notice that his clothes and hair were soaked in blood. He saw us standing there, turned and tried to walk away casually as if nothing was going on. He looked very pale and a bit unsteady on his feet. I called on him to stop just as he slumped to the ground sliding down the fire escape wall. I left a suspicious Merlin in a sit and approached the semi-conscious man. I had a look at his arm which had been sliced to the bone and was bleeding profusely. I asked him what had happened and he answered in a very heavy Russian accent, 'Nothing officer, I fell down some stairs.'

'What, about seven thousand of the buggers mate?' He didn't say another thing.

I called for an ambulance and told the police from Chatswood what had happened when they arrived a few minutes later. There were four other fire escapes to cover and I wasn't sure if the others had been used while I was there on my own. We kept a guard on the injured man and went up to the twentieth floor via the lift.

There were four other officers, myself and Merlin. Not knowing what to expect, I got one of the officers to knock on the door and move back behind me and Merlin with the others. The door was opened by a shirtless man who was also covered in blood and had one of the most battered and bruised faces I had ever seen. He also had a very thick Russian accent. All he said was, 'It's about time officers, everyone is down here.' Then he turned and walked back down the hallway. The hallway I might add was splattered in blood literally from the floor up the walls and even on the ceiling. I had never seen this amount of blood splattered over such a wide area in my life. (Not even at Long Bay Prison before I joined the police.) I held Merlin on a very short lead and followed the bloody mess down to the lounge room. If I thought the hallway was bad then the lounge room was absolutely horrendous. The whole room was again splattered in blood and every single stick of furniture had been smashed, from the coffee table to the television. Sitting in the middle were two terrified young ladies and an unconscious man who looked like he had been battered from pillar to post with a pickaxe handle. The two girls were jabbering in what sounded like Russian and crying at the same time.

As the other police piled in and started to find out exactly what had happened, I searched the rest of the unit with Merlin who, like me, I think could not believe what he was seeing. Everything in every room was destroyed and/or covered in blood. I went to the balcony and looked over where I saw another large smear of blood which had covered the paintwork. It was like something out of a bad horror movie. The unconscious man, it turned out, was the same person I had seen hanging from the balcony. The bleeding man from the fire escape was his mate who had been slashed and stabbed in an effort to defend his mate on the balcony. He had left the unit in a vain attempt to catch the attackers who it turns out were rivals in the drug trade. This information was by no means forthcoming that night. None of them wanted to tell the police anything. The information was given about a week later by one of the people who were in the unit that night. Just goes to show that the violent dark side of the drug trade is not limited to dingy inner city hovels. All the ugliness that goes with it can surface anywhere, anytime with crooks from any part of the world right here in Australia.

Heavy Scent

I had received a phone call about half way through a shift that was going nowhere. There was absolutely nothing happening anywhere. I had been asked to get over to Kings Cross Police Station for a special job the details of which I was to keep to myself. Kings Cross is Sydney's red light district which is open twenty four hours a day. I perked up a bit hoping that we would be able to get out and do something this shift and turned up at the inner city station about half an hour later. It was hard to find a parking spot as all the police parking had been taken up with a couple of police buses and various other police vehicles along with others I didn't recognise. I walked into the station leaving Merlin to enjoy the sights of Kings Cross from the back of the car.

The muster room was full of about fifty people including police officers in both plain clothes and uniform. Also present were officers from the Department of Immigration. We were going to assist them in a search of all the local brothels for illegal sex workers. This is a big problem with young girls being recruited by crime syndicates overseas with the promise of work and big money in Australia. The problem is that the work ends up being in brothels and most of the money goes to the criminals who are holding these unfortunate peoples' passports until their 'debt' has been paid. Their debt usually means they have to pay back air fares and living expenses, but none of this is explained to them until it's too late and they are trapped in the sex trade.

The immigration officers had conducted such an operation about six months earlier with limited success. They had found out that some of the sex workers had been hidden behind false walls while the officers searched in vain. It was going to be our job to search the brothels after everyone had been removed making sure no one was left behind.

About an hour after the briefing we turned up en masse at the first illegal brothel. After our undercover officers had been invited in, they would hold the door open for the uniforms to pile in. This would cause total mayhem inside the establishment with naked men and women frantically trying to get dressed and explain why they were there. It was quite a scene to behold. After fifteen minutes or so, everyone was cleared out and it was time for Merlin to do his thing. After watching all the excitement and hearing all the shouting from the rear of the car, he was ready to go and needed little in the way of encouragement when we reached the door. I still yelled out, 'Police, come out or I'll send the dog.' Merlin barked and tried to drag me in there so I released him from his lead with a command and watched as he darted inside the den of iniquity which, despite popular opinion, was a very clean and tidy place. I followed him in, watching his body language as he entered and cleared every single room and common passageway. Nothing in here.

The next place wasn't very far away and the initial phase went much the same as the first establishment. There was one difference that made me change the way I was going to use Merlin. One of the enforcers who was sitting on the stash of cash inside one of the offices had been armed with a handgun. I decided that just in case there were more I'd leave Merlin on his lead and conduct the search with him. We waited until everyone was out then moved to the entrance. As I would have direct control over Merlin and I didn't want anyone who might be hiding inside with a gun to know we were coming, I didn't give a verbal challenge. We entered, moving as quietly as we could and being as thorough as possible. There was a reception area with an office and two-way mirror behind it. The hallway led off with five rooms off to either side of that. At the very end of the hallway was a dark room with a lounge and spa inside. We checked each of the ten rooms off the hallway with nothing but the scent left behind by the girls, clients and searching police and immigration officers. We moved up to the spa room where Merlin started to puff up and raise the hackles on his back. I told him he was a good boy and gave the room the once over myself, even checking in the spa. There was nothing I could see. I let Merlin off his lead and gave him a command. He jumped up onto the couch which ran along two of the walls in the room. He put his head over the back of the couch and came up two seconds later with a mouthful of lingerie and bras, shaking them from side to side. I looked down and realised he had found the dirty laundry basket! Yuck, but I still laughed. I tried to get him to drop the soiled garments but he was enjoying the heavy, dirty scent too much. I ended up putting on my rubber gloves and taking them out of his mouth. I remember thinking 'I don't get paid enough for this'. I moved the basket out of the room as I didn't think that his initial reaction when we entered the room was for the laundry basket.

I put him on his lead and ran him along the couch. Bingo, he stopped and snapped his head in the direction of the wall behind the lounge again. I gave him a 'good boy' hoping it wasn't more underwear and pulled the lounge away from the wall expecting someone to be underneath it. Instead I saw a hatch 1m high and 1.5m wide on the wall. It was painted the same colour as the wall and unless you were as close as we were it was very hard to see. Merlin was barking and scratching at the door, knocking it in as he tried to see who was in there. I pulled his straining body back and yelled out, 'Police, come out here now, I know you're in there.'

Not long after, a young girl wearing only underwear came out followed by a very nervous and naked middle-aged man who was sweating profusely.

Merlin barked and salivated as I made them sit on the lounge and called in the other officers. One of the officers told me that he had found a set of clothes in one of the rooms but no owner. I was very happy with Merlin who had managed to pick out these two behind a hidden hatch in the wall even though this place was packed with heavy and recent scent from the other occupants and visitors. It still amazes me that he does this for me time and time again.

Cannabis Crop

On occasion, we go away with the Drug Squad as part of the Cannabis Eradication Program. These are usually carried out on the state's mid-north and far-north coast where the climate is perfect for the cultivation of this illegal plant. On this particular trip, we met up with the Drug Squad and stayed at one of the larger towns in resort-style accommodation. There were also police from the radio electronics unit to help with communications and a police helicopter and support staff. In all, there were about twenty officers and ten vehicles, including two dirt bikes.

The Drug Squad guys would come armed with intelligence gathered throughout the year on the best areas we should search to find the crops. The police helicopter was to be used to locate crops throughout the area, map them and guide us in to destroy them. The cannabis crops are coloured a very distinctive green which sticks out from everything around them. They are hard to see from ground level in these areas as the tropical forest areas are so thick. The only way to do it is from the air.

I was given an unmarked Dog Squad four-wheel drive and was quite looking forward to the change of scenery the next week was going to bring. It was going to be our job to search the crop locations and hunt down anyone who might run from them. The only problem with this is that the police helicopter is a bit obvious and just about all the cannabis growers know that its presence will soon bring more police swarming in to take all the happiness out of their day.

The first day we moved into the Port Macquarie hinterland which consists of very steep and rugged mountains covered in thick tropical forest. The convoy moved out at 6am turning off the highway and straight up a very narrow dirt track which I would never have known was there if I hadn't been following the Drug Squad. Merlin was being bounced and pitched inside his cage and I knew he probably wasn't having as much fun as I was driving the four-wheel drive over this difficult terrain. Just as we reached the peak of the first range and headed down into a very deep valley, the police helicopter came in low following the terrain towards our first target which was a hippie commune about 2km from where we were. The helicopter reported that there were about ten people all on horseback riding into the forest out of the commune. It wasn't long before the crew rather despondently reported losing sight of them under the thick canopy. The two Drug Squad trail bikes took off ahead in a blaze of exhaust smoke and dirt whipped up by the tyres. They tried in vain to find the horses but local knowledge and a big head start allowed them to disappear without trace. Even if Merlin and I started a search I didn't think either of us were going to outrun or outstay a galloping horse.

We reached the commune which was about six little hovels and lean-tos bunched together in a clearing. I let a grateful Merlin out of the truck and set him off for a search while the drug guys watched. Merlin went into each little hovel indicating that someone had just been there. He started to search in an ever-widening circle as his search went on. Just as I was about to call him back, he spotted two wallabies which saw him at the same time and bounded away. Merlin didn't hesitate and was off for the chase. I yelled out 'no' but it was too late, the little bastard wasn't going to let this opportunity go. He disappeared in about two seconds and was gone. I looked back at the Drug Squad officers who were looking at me and shaking their heads. What could I do except swear under my breath and start calling for my alleged mate. Like I've said before, dogs can make you look like a champion or they can make you look like an idiot. This was one of those 'magical idiot' moments. Half an hour later, with my voice box dying from overuse and my frustration level at maximum, Merlin emerged from the heavy undergrowth panting heavily, covered in dirt and foliage. I just stared at him and had to hold my temper at bay. He came towards me with his head down and eyes averted. He knew he was in trouble and that I was, to say the least, cranky with him. I wrestled a bit more with my anger and told him to get in the car. He slinked over and jumped in. I was just glad that he was back and hadn't been injured or completely lost. I gave him a much-needed drink then slammed the door shut.

By this time, the Drug Squad guys had cleared the buildings and surrounds, taking about fifty mature cannabis plants and some dry leaf bags with them. They had left about five minutes before Merlin's return from his hunting expedition. I had to hustle along the dirt track to catch up for the next search at another commune about 10km along the valley.

I must have hit just about every bump and ditch along the way which threw Merlin every which way in the back. I was secretly happy with the rough road as it made me feel I was getting some payback. Childish perhaps, but it made me feel better.

Luckily I came up behind the last four-wheel drive in the convoy just as they were heading in. It was a re-run of the first entry and search with the occupants taking off into the heavy rain forest. I searched again with Merlin who was a bit second-hand after his first run and consequent drive. I stayed very close and didn't give him any opportunity to go for the scenic tour again. There were no bodies but plenty of mature cannabis plants which on average were 2–3m high!

This went on for the next couple of days culminating at the end of the week with a hike into very rugged terrain where we found another crop site. We ended up having to climb down a cliff using a rope and ladder which the cannabis growers had left there. It was quite an intricate operation with a complete irrigation system and some booby traps laid around the crop. Merlin was left tied to a tree at the top of the rope ladder. This would ensure that anyone who came along to cut the rope and trap us would not be able to do so. The police helicopter was used to ferry the plants out on its cargo net. We loaded eight nets of about twenty mature plants and by the time we climbed the cliff and destroyed the irrigation system, I was totally spent and glad to head back to our accommodation. By the end of the week, the Drug Squad had charged about ten people with drug-related offences and had taken enough plants to fill a very large truck which followed us to every job. We had not really ended up doing any good dog jobs, but it had been great to be out in the wilderness and ruining some of the drug dealers' crops.

Copper

There's one kind of precious metal that's just about everywhere and is never locked up in a safe or watched by armed guards. It's found in abandoned buildings, building sites and power stations. It also brings in big dollars from scrap metal dealers. It's copper, found in most wiring especially on large commercial sites where large amounts of electricity run day and night. The thieves who target it are taking massive risks but as usual they believe the risks are worth the payout. On this particular night it was not only the risk of electrocution for the thieves, but running the gauntlet of a certain black-and-tan dog that was going to shut down their little enterprise.

It was about midnight and we had been called to Greenacre in Sydney's south-west, just off the Hume Highway. The police from Bankstown had seen a car which was wanted for stealing commercial amounts of copper wiring from a State Rail repair depot a few nights earlier, parked up beside a large electricity sub-station. The car engine was still hot and some movement had been seen inside the barbed wire compound. There were a number of buildings and areas full of long grass within the complex and most were separated by further wire fences in between. Most worrying of all for me and Merlin were the multitude of 'Danger, High Voltage' signs throughout the complex. I spoke to the Bankstown supervisor who told me a good perimeter had been set so I could go in with my dog and search. It's amazing how good the perimeters are and how keen the other police are for you to do the searches when it's in places like this. I was just about to start my 'on lead' search with Merlin who was quite oblivious to the extreme danger inside the search area when one of the Sydney Electricity engineers arrived with a set of keys and, more importantly, knowledge of the complex. He agreed to come in with me and point out the areas that were out of bounds. As much as I want to catch the crooks, there's no point in either me or Merlin dying over copper theft.

After opening the first gate, Merlin picked something up straight away. He puffed up and started to wag his tail then dragged me towards a cyclone wire fence into long grass. We went back and forth along it until he shot through a freshly cut hole at the base. Easy for my partner, not easy for a man of my dimensions. A few swear words later and I was through, being dragged along on my hands and knees until Merlin came to a sudden halt growling and barking at the first crook who was curled up in a ball praying that this was all just a bad dream. I jumped up and shone my torch on this motionless little crook that would not look up. I said to him, 'Mate, it's the police, I'm not going away, you've been busted, just get up.' Nothing. He wouldn't budge or acknowledge our presence. After a few more attempts at trying to convince him unsuccessfully with reason and conversation, I was running out of patience. He wouldn't even move when Merlin was barking about 2cm from his ear just about drowning him in the dog slobber which was drooling across his cheek. I couldn't believe this guy. There was only one thing to do. I held Merlin on a very short lead and picked the thief up by the scruff of his neck. All of a sudden he looked at me and stood up. The best he could come up with was, 'What's happening, I was having a sleep in the grass.' I then pointed out to him that people don't usually come into electrical sub stations to have a sleep and they certainly don't do it with a tool belt around their waists wearing black clothing and backpacks. Further, 'would you stick to that story because I'd love to see you front up to a court and use it as your excuse.' To this day I can't believe crooks that get caught red-handed use these lame excuses and, even worse, they get crabby when we don't believe them! I called in two of the perimeter police who placed him under arrest then marched him and his array of sleeping equipment out of the complex. They just laughed as he pleaded the same case to them.

Now it was time for number two. During the first arrest some of the perimeter police had seen and heard further movement near one of the fences which ran up behind a car dealership on the highway. Merlin had by now stopped barking at the first crook so I walked him back towards the fence line and started to get him focussed for the next search. I got his attention and started banging on the fence. He lost interest in everything else and started to focus on the next job at hand. The fence line consisted of a cyclone wire fence topped with barbed wire. There was only about a metre between it and the rear of the car yard which consisted of a 5m-high solid brick wall. The whole thing was 50–60m long and some of the base was completely covered in long grass and undergrowth. We started at one end which had a new hole cut in the base of the cyclone wire. I yelled out, 'Police, come out or I'll send the dog.' Merlin barked and pulled at the lead. He was pumped and eager to get moving He was showing me that he knew there was someone there and he wanted to show me where. I yelled the challenge out again and Merlin kept building himself up into his searching frenzy. I slipped him off his lead and gave him a command. He speared off down the narrow corridor at breakneck speed. I crouched over and started to move in the same direction, constantly getting snagged on the fence and vegetation. Unfortunately about 30m in, the passage became so narrow I was unable to get any further and turning around was not really an option either. Just at that same moment I shone the torch down the passage and saw that Merlin had found someone and was standing on top of him barking. I told him he was a good boy and recalled him to where I was stuck. I saw the crook sit up and look back at us. I was a little concerned to see a long screwdriver in his hand. I yelled out at him, 'Drop that weapon and walk out here right now.'

He looked at me and I could tell he was weighing up his options. I yelled again, 'Mate, there's no escape, drop the weapon and come out this way.' He dropped the screwdriver and started to come in our direction. I backed up and had to drag Merlin with me as he was keeping an eye on the crook as we moved. Just as I was able to stand in a crouch I looked back and saw the crook scaling up a drain pipe on the brick wall. I gave Merlin an appropriate command and let him off his lead. The last thing we wanted was to have this guy running on roofs and out on to the highway—for all I knew he was still armed. I had confidence that even if he was, Merlin would be able to take care of him in this confined space.

Merlin shot back up the passage like a rat in a drainpipe. He jumped up and managed to get hold of the crook by the rear pocket of his jeans holding on with his top and bottom canines. The crook kept on climbing. I wasn't sure what he was going to do when he reached the top with a police dog attached to his trousers but I was keen to find out. But gravity and bad stitching combined causing the jeans pocket to detach with Merlin still holding on dutifully. He came crashing to the ground falling about a metre and a half onto his hind legs. He recovered straight away and began jumping and snapping in an attempt to arrest the climbing felon who had by now reached the roof disappearing from our sight. I had conveyed the turn of events over

191

the police radio. I recalled Merlin and with great difficulty extricated myself from the fence line. Merlin was looking up at the roof where we could hear the desperate crook running back and forth along the tin sheets. He no doubt could see all the police surrounding him but was trying to find an escape route anyway. I went to the northern end of the building and waited. Merlin sat next to me staring up at the roof and occasionally barking at the noise. It didn't take long for the crook to realise what was happening and how pointless his efforts were. He came to our end of the building and shimmied down the drain pipe. He was met at the bottom by police bearing handcuffs, accompanied by Merlin's growl-and-bark routine. Both men were charged with breaking and entering and received lengthy gaol terms after a large stash of copper pipe was found at both their houses.

The Ultimate Test

This was one of the biggest jobs the Dog Squad had ever seen. I had been contacted by detectives from a task force looking into extortion and standover tactics in the supply of hair care products (who would have thought that could happen in this industry?).

The background was that a certain supplier was trying to drive out his competition by firebombing their warehouses and offices in New South Wales.

I attended a briefing at the old Chatswood Police Station with the task force detectives who explained that they had identified the ringleader and the thugs he had employed to carry out his dirty work. They had surveillance police following them and were listening to all their calls via phone taps. The consensus was that they were going to kneecap a businessman at his warehouse located in Chatswood using baseball bats. They were probably going to firebomb the warehouse after they had dealt with him.

I started to think maybe I was going to need some help with this one. The area we had to cover was large and complex with many avenues of escape open to anyone who decided they didn't want to co-operate. Luckily, a very good mate of mine in the section, Duncan, was on-duty that shift with his dog, Kaiser. Both had gone through their initial training with me and Merlin. I rang him and gave him the gist of the job, promising him some excitement if the crooks turned up. As it was, he won a toss and chose to be right in close to the action and able to use Kaiser to arrest them. I have always been a rotten gambler so it was no surprise that I had to cover the outer part of the complex. Soon enough we all set off to lay the trap—it was 8pm on a warm summer evening. The warehouse was inside a complex in Short Street. There was a two-storey car park with the warehouses offset and below it on another two levels. The target, (let's call him John Smith) of the proposed knee-capping was contacted and had the situation explained to him. To say he was absolutely gobsmacked with what he had been told would be the understatement of the century. He left and was replaced by two detectives from the task force who took up residence in his office. Duncan and Kaiser were directly across from the warehouse in an office with three other detectives. I was hidden in an underground car park about 100m up another road which was directly opposite the entrance to the complex. There were also about ten more detectives secreted around the area in buildings and cars waiting for the moment the crooks turned up and went to work.

Usually with jobs like this, we wait for hours on end, seldom getting a result for one reason or another. As it was, the police tailing the crooks had lost them. This is not unusual as proper surveillance is one of the hardest things you can try especially if the crooks are on edge heading to a job. What we did have is access to their phones and this confirmed that they were on the way to Chatswood to 'take care of business'.

I was a little despondent being so far from the warehouse, but I really thought that these guys would turn up, be confronted by Duncan and Kaiser, then give up. Little did I know that this was definitely not going to be the case.

About an hour into waiting the encrypted secret squirrel radio burst into life. 'Everybody stand by, the target vehicle has turned up, get ready to move on my command.' The crooks had turned up in a car which one of them owned. They circled the block apparently in an attempt to make sure there was no one around. Instead there were about twenty sets of eyes watching everything they did. They parked their car in a dark industrial driveway about 100m from the complex entrance. Two of them got out while the third stayed with the car. They walked casually up to the car park entrance. One of them walked up the ramp and disappeared from sight on the top level overlooking the warehouse entrance. The second man, wearing a heavy military coat, continued into the complex and headed straight up to the warehouse office door. He looked over his shoulder then knocked.

One of the detectives answered, being careful to open only the glass door and not the security grill which remained locked. The crook asked if he was John Smith. The detective answered that yes, he was. Then, in a split second without saying a word, the crook pulled out a sawn-off .22 calibre bolt-action rifle and fired it at the detective's leg. Thank God he missed, but when I spoke to this detective afterwards he told me he felt the bullet pass his right knee. He is a very, very lucky man.

This immediately set Duncan and Kaiser into action. As the bad guy tried to re-cock his rifle, Dunc and Kaiser burst out from the office doorway and ran straight at the shooter who turned and faced them, raised a now reloaded rifle and fired a shot directly at them from about 5m, somehow missing again. He started to run back up the driveway towards my position.

I had heard the first crack, thinking it was a petrol bomb going off. I grabbed my dog's lead and started to run towards the driveway. I remember looking down the driveway to see the offender in the overcoat running towards me. At this point he was about 100m from where Merlin and I were running. From this point on, everything seemed to happen in slow motion. I had heard the second crack before I saw the offender. It still had not registered with me that this lunatic was actually shooting at police officers. I can still feel the massive shot of adrenalin when I saw him turn back towards Duncan and Kaiser who were chasing him 'on lead' and were only about 3m away when he fired another shot right in his face—I still cannot believe it missed him. I was by now about 20m from the action and drew my service pistol from the holster.

I saw that Duncan was still running at the crook, who was still running towards me. The crook had not yet seen me because he was trying to chamber another round in his rifle by working the action. I heard Duncan yell something and release Kaiser from his lead. I saw Kaiser's ears go back and watched as his legs pumped him towards this bad guy at 110 per cent power. The words screamed by the crook who was unsuccessfully trying to chamber another round. The sight of Kaiser launching at him with jaws open and mouth salivating will be stuck with me until the day I die. 'I give up,' the crook yelled, dropping the rifle at his feet. Well, buddy boy, it was way too late for that. At this close range and with the lead up to his release, there was nothing that was going to stop Kaiser from carrying out his mission. I have seen a lot of hits by police dogs both in training and for real, but this was the biggest, most violent hit by a dog I have ever witnessed. This crook was six foot one and about 110kg. Kaiser hit his arm at full speed and just about swallowed it. He hit with such a force that the shooter was knocked off his feet and hit the ground like a sack of cement thrown from a second-floor window. I can still see the spray of sweat being thrown from him as the dog hit. This was not the end of it either. Kaiser held onto his arm and just kept biting down harder and harder, the more he tried to struggle away. This was lucky in a way for the crook because, as I said, I had drawn my pistol and had it aimed at him; I had made the decision to shoot but had stopped because he was directly between myself and Duncan. If I had missed I would probably have hit Dunc or one of the other detectives running with him.

Much later in court I was giving my evidence with this same criminal sitting opposite. For some strange reason he was constantly sniggering and making stupid faces at me. That was until I was asked under cross-examination why I drew my pistol and aimed it at the offender. I looked straight at him making eye contact and said straight at him, 'I was going to shoot him, the only thing that saved him was the fact that there were police directly behind him otherwise I was definitely going to shoot him.' I can tell you that this wiped the smile off his face as he finally realised the gravity of his situation and how close he came to dying that night.

Also after the hit that Kaiser put on there was really no need, thank God. Duncan ran straight in without any hesitation and jumped onto the crook who by now knew the game was up. He was sobbing and pleading to have the dog taken away.

There were, however, a couple more things to take care of. First, the driver of the getaway car had seen police come from everywhere and tried to take off. His path had been blocked by detectives in an undercover vehicle. He had a go anyway, flooring his car and driving onto a garden. Unfortunately for him, this was a lovely Australian native garden with natural rocks placed all through it. He drove straight over one such rock, becoming stuck and spinning his wheels. After a short and violent struggle which involved police smashing his car window and forcibly removing him through the same, he was taken into custody kicking and screaming.

Second, there was the matter of the third guy that had gone to the upper level of the car park. I had one of the other detectives call out to me to come with him to find this last offender. Duncan definitely had things under control so I started up the steep driveway towards the top level. I had Merlin by my side and two detectives following behind. We were about half way up the 100m-long drive when I saw a crouching figure come down from an adjoining roof and onto our drive. He was stooped over and looking back over his shoulder into the car park. Amazingly he had not seen us. I bent into a crouch and picked up the pace hoping to be on top of him before he saw us but he looked down in our direction with about 20m still between us.

I yelled, 'Police, don't move' and immediately the hairy one started to bark and pull me in his direction. It seemed he didn't want Kaiser to be the only one having the fun. The crook ran, so I released Merlin and gave him a command. He shot off straight at him as fast as he could go.

The last crook was running in the direction of the car park. He climbed over a short barrier fence which I knew had a sheer drop of about 8–10m onto a concrete driveway below it. I remember quite vividly yelling, 'Don't be bloody stupid mate, just give up.' As the area was very well lit, I saw him ease himself over and hold onto the barrier fence which was made of metal. It was then I realised that if I didn't call off Merlin then he was going to go over the edge as well. I yelled a command and he put on the brakes, turning and trotting back to me while looking over his shoulder at his recent target.

It was then that I saw why he was hanging there by one hand. He was reaching into the front of his pants. About one second later he produced an automatic 9mm handgun and about half a second after this, he lost his grip and disappeared from sight. I heard a very loud crashing sound then a sickening thud. He had fallen the full 8–10m and landed on a plastic wheelie bin, before landing heavily on the concrete and losing hold of the handgun. Even though I believed that this guy was going to try and shoot me, I immediately called over the radio for an ambulance. I could see that he was not moving and was going to have serious injuries if he was still alive. Luckily, there were two detectives already hiding down there. They had seen the whole incident as it had unfolded. They took over and waited until the ambos turned up.

All this from the first shot fired to the last bad guy falling from the building had taken about 45 seconds. It just goes to show how much can happen in a short period of time when the action starts. Both the armed offenders in this case ended up in hospital. The shooter had some very deep lacerations down to the bone from where Kaiser had nailed him. The second man that fell had numerous broken bones and internal injuries. Both received lengthy gaol terms as a result of their actions in this incident.

I can still remember seeing Duncan right after it had finished. I shook my head and said to him, 'You wanted action, I gave you action, don't ever say I never give you anything.'

He just looked at me, shook his head and smiled.

Even though it wasn't me or my dog directly involved, I was privileged to have been a part of this incident because it was definitely the ultimate test for a police dog team. For his part, Duncan was awarded a Police Valour medal, the highest award for bravery a police officer can receive and Duncan's second. I was awarded a Commissioner's Commendation for Bravery, my second of those. I know that these awards are not the motivation for either Duncan or myself but it's nice to be recognised for the work we do.

Merlin is now five years old and right in the prime of his working life. He's been around a long time and encountered a lot of different situations and people. He is still young enough to get around and do his job very well. Merlin has probably got three to four years of working left in him barring any injuries or illnesses. When it comes time to retire him he'll go to the backyard and take it easy. He will have earned it by then.

I think I'll have the biggest problem with his retirement, as he has been such a big part of my life for such a long time. I still love what I do for a living and wouldn't change it for anything in the world. Like I said at the start, there isn't a day that goes by that I don't want to put Merlin in the car and go out on the road.

The Worst Day of My Life

It has been almost two years since I wrote the last paragraph. I have not been able to get the words down. The following events occurred not long after having written that particular chapter. I had always known that this day would come, but I never really wanted to believe it could. The worst day of my life was coming and it was going to knock me down for the count. It had all started two weeks beforehand during our annual accreditation. Merlin was in the agility compound. He had just cleared the hurdles and was starting up the ladder and plank. This requires him to climb up a steep ladder, walk along a wooden plank then walk down another plank to the ground at the other end. As he climbed the ladder I noticed that he was struggling and was actually pulling himself up the steps with his chin. Each step was causing him a lot of pain—he was straining and using all his strength to drag himself up. He was whining and grunting with each step he climbed; I knew it must have been agony because he never usually showed pain. It is a sign of weakness and therefore vulnerability for pack animals. Such was his desire to please me and make it over, he just kept going.

I took him off and stopped the exercise immediately. Merlin was in pain and couldn't move his hind legs properly. At the time, I thought he'd pulled a muscle or thrown out his vertebrae. A couple of muscle relaxants and he'll be fine, I thought. So the next day we went to our vet. A night of rest and he looked much better. I really wasn't concerned at all; a quick x-ray and maybe a week's rest then back to work.

Unfortunately the look on the vet's face said it all. He came straight out and told me that Merlin's working days were over. He had a problem with his spine and was going to be in constant pain. To explain what this meant he showed me the x-ray. Basically it looked as though Merlin's spine had been hit with a hammer leaving a large dent in the shape of a V. He could have an operation, the outcome of which was not guaranteed and even if successful he would never work again and would not be able to move without a certain amount of pain. He then told me that the best thing for him was probably to put him down. He may as well have taken those last words and hammered them through my forehead with a chisel. I couldn't believe what I was hearing. I mean, kill my best mate!

My first reaction was 'No way, I want a second opinion'. But I knew deep down that he was right. If I was to keep Merlin alive and have him live out his days in my backyard he would have been miserable. He was used to getting out and about at work, not being caged up in a yard. Worst of all, he would have to watch me with another dog leaving for work while he stayed at home. Other handlers have done this and 99.99 per cent of the dogs have gone downhill very fast. They become depressed and resentful. They lose weight and develop medical problems very fast. The only reason I was going to keep him from being put down was for myself, not for his wellbeing. I tried thinking up ways of getting him out of it. I considered an offer from a very well meaning sergeant from a local police station. She had a friend who would take him onto his farm. Initially I thought this might be the answer but the reality of the situation was that Merlin was a trained police dog who was capable of doing a huge amount of damage to people and property. He would listen to me but anybody else from outside the squad who tried to control him was in for a trip to the hospital.

I absolutely hated myself but I knew I had to bite the bullet and do what was ultimately best for my mate. At the time I came to that decision, I felt like such a total bastard that I couldn't even look at myself in the mirror.

The next problem was how could I bring myself to physically take him there and watch while they put him to sleep. I couldn't and God knows I would be in no fit state to drive home after. I decided not to take him myself. I wanted my last memory of Merlin to be of him happy and chasing a ball at the oval, not lying on a slab at the vets with his tongue hanging out of a lifeless body. One of the boys from the section came by on the day. I had taken him around our favourite oval and walking track and played with his favourite toy, a big rubber bone. He was limping and moving very slowly when we came through the front gate and into the yard for the last time. I went out to the backyard and put Merlin into his lead for the last time. I knelt down and put my arm around his neck. I got a lovely wet tongue in my ear while I said, 'See ya mate, thanks for everything, I'll catch you on the other side.'

I walked him out and helped him into the car. His back was really bad by now and getting up even that short distance was hard for him. The poor bugger thought we were going to work and was wagging his tail and looking out the side window.

I went back inside and completely lost my composure. I make no secret of the fact that I sat in the lounge room with his lead in my hands and cried for about an hour. I felt guilty and incredibly empty. I just sat there with my face in my hands feeling like Judas.

About 2pm that day I received a call saying that he was gone and out of pain. My mate was gone.

I spent the next months feeling very low and alone. I tried to convince myself he was lying on his back in heaven eating sausages and sleeping on a big heated mattress. RIP Merlin.

What Now?

I was absolutely devastated for the first month. I took three months' long service leave because I just couldn't face up to being with another dog. In fact, I wasn't even interested in having another dog. I even started to think about leaving the Squad, not wanting to have to go through the ordeal of losing another good mate.

I started to train for the Tactical Operations Unit selection course. The hard training sessions I was putting myself through helped take my mind off thinking about Merlin even though to this very day I think about him and the jobs we did together at least once every single day. At the age of thirty-seven, I was competing with police officers at least ten to fifteen years younger than me.

I attended what's called the barrier day where they measure your level of physical fitness and strength. We were made to do chin-ups, dips, sit-ups, sprints, and a swim in overalls in Sydney Harbour culminating in a run and dummy carry. All this pain dished out with the beautiful backdrop of Sydney Harbour. I can proudly say that I was not sent home early from the day like some of the others were because they couldn't complete the tasks. Mind you I was nowhere near at the top and woke up the next day feeling every one of my thirty-seven years old. It turns out I need not have bothered as I was not selected to go any further. In spite of this I wasn't all that concerned; I was starting to think about another dog and was missing not having one around. I was also missing not being around the boys from the Squad even though most of them are insane.

I went and saw the commander who said he was glad I had come to my senses and decided to stay. At the time we were not running any training courses and did not have any new dogs to train but I was given a dog from a retired handler for about six months until a training course was available. I looked at a number of dogs and trained with a few. One of them failed at tracking as he couldn't concentrate for more than 100m. Another one I didn't like, I just couldn't get along with him and just plain disliked him.

Finally I was given a chance with Rex, a 40kg German shepherd who was very similar looking to Merlin. He was donated and was at the time a very immature and flighty style of a dog. I saw great potential in him and he had a very dominant and strong-willed streak in him. I started to train him but had a very hard time doing so. I was used to Merlin who did things in his own special way. I now had to adjust to a completely different dog who was going to do things his way.

Towards the end of his career Merlin would be doing 90 per cent of the work with only 10 per cent coming from me. Now I had to turn completely around and it was me doing 90 per cent of the work and only 10 per cent from Rex. I was back where I had started five years before. I am proud to be part of a squad which has a unique and respected role within the police force, however, and will hang in there with Rex. No dog will ever be able to replace Merlin and I will never forget him, but life goes on and so does the fight against crime.

First published in Australia in 2009 by
New Holland Publishers (Australia) Pty Ltd
Sydney • Auckland • London • Cape Town

1/66 Gibbes Street Chatswood NSW 2067 Australia
218 Lake Road Northcote Auckland New Zealand
86 Edgware Road London W2 2EA United Kingdom
80 McKenzie Street Cape Town 8001 South Africa

A record of this book is held at the National Library of Australia

ISBN 9781741108354

Publisher: Linda Williams
Publishing Manager: Lliane Clarke
Senior Project Editor: Joanna Tovia
Designer: Hayley Norman
Production Manager: Olga Dementiev
Printer: McPherson's Printing Group, Maryborough, Victoria

10 9 8 7 6 5 4 3 2 1

Photographic credits: Mike Combe and Mark Baxter
Cover photo: Getty Images